Unlocking the Expert In You!

Avery Thompson

Contents

Unlocking The Expert In You!...1
What Is An Expert?..5
    Experts Know More about Their Topic than Most..6
    Experts Innovate..6
    Experts Are Who Others Turn To For Advice..6
    Teachers, Coaches, Mentors, and Consultants 7
    Becoming an Expert Will Serve You for a Lifetime 8
    Experts Never Stop Learning and Growing...9
    Revisiting the Word "Expert" 11
It's Easier than You Think to Become an Expert 13
Your Purpose for Becoming an Expert..17
What Will You Become An Expert On? 20
    What to Do If You Already Know What You Want To Become an Expert On.....20
    What to Do If You Don't Have Any Ideas for Your Expertise..............................21
    Choosing Your Topic...21
    What to Do If You're Totally Stuck for Ideas 23
    Moving Forward With Your Topic..23
Gathering the Knowledge You Need...25
    Setting Yourself Up For Success...26
    More on Reading Books..27
Don't Just Read— Practice 30
    Start Writing about What You're Learning...31
    Trying and Doing 33
    Interact With Other Experts...33
    Make Mistakes and Learn From Them..34
    Be Mindful of What You're Doing and Why...36
Other Experts Will Help You Get To Where You Want To Be Much More Quickly.37
    Why..37
    How 37
    Learn From the Best..39
    Learn What Worked For Them and What Didn't 40
    What to Look For In Other Experts..40
Reflect Along the Way..42
Develop Your Weekly Expertise Schedule 45

- Getting Started With Your Plan 46

Getting People to Look At You as an Expert 50

- Don't Just Look Like an Expert 51
- Treat People Well 51
- Stand Out From Other Experts 52
- Give More Than You Receive 52
- Have Other People's Best Interests at Heart 53
- Never Get Too Big 53

What to Do When You're First Getting Started: a Recap of the First Steps to Expertise 55

- Networking as an Expert 57
- Marketing Yourself as an Expert 59
  - Creating a Website or Blog as an Expert 60
  - Being Present on Social Media 61
  - Facebook 62
  - LinkedIn 63
  - Pinterest and Instagram— 63
  - Writing Books and Creating Content 63
  - Speaking at Seminars 66
  - Associate with Other Experts 66

Your Plan for Marketing Yourself as an Expert 68
Use Your Expertise to Create Your Own Opportunities 69

- Forming Your Own Business as an Expert 69
- Consult for High-End Clients 71
- Freelance 71
- Become a Coach 72
- Teach 73
- Invent 73
- Create More Than One Opportunity for Yourself 74

Struggles You Might Have on Your Journey to Become an Expert 75
Becoming an Expert on More Than One Thing 78
Your 30 Day Get Started Plan: Become an Expert in 30 Days 79

- Day 1: Find Your Topic 79
- Day 2: Create Your Plan 80
- Day 3: Locate Your Materials 80
- Read 81
- Listen 82

- Watch 82
- Network 82
- Create 82
- Day 4: Set Yourself Up For Automated Success 82
- Blogs 82
- Alerts 82
- Accountability 83
- Day 5 through 29: This Is Your Daily Plan to Follow 83
- Goals- 83
- Read- 83
- Listen- 83
- Watch- 84
- Network- 84
- Create 84
- Day 30: 84

What to Do After 30 Days Is Over 85

- Adjusting Your Goals along the Way 85
- Keeping Your Reason Why at the Top of Your Mind 85
- Keeping the Passion Alive For Your Topic 86
- Your Journey Is Just Getting Started 86

What Is an Expert?

We all have an idea in our mind of what makes an expert. For most of us, the idea of becoming one ourselves seems somewhat unattainable. Those "experts" are way too far out of reach for the average person, right? They're the people who eat, sleep, and breathe their topic. They've spent a lifetime getting to where they are. That kind of success, that kind of expertise, is untouchable.

But I challenge you to think about what expertise really is. What does it *really* mean to be an expert? Do you have to be near the grave after a lifetime of study before you can be considered an expert? Do you really need to spend 10,000 hours studying something to be an expert about it? I don't think so— I think that's very far from the truth, actually.

I'll even go as far as to say that I believe anyone can become an expert on any topic. In many cases, you can achieve a certain level of expertise in as little as a month. It's time to change your mind set about expertise. If you want to become an expert on a topic, you can.

We're going to talk a lot about why you want to become an expert and what you hope to achieve. There has to be a benefit waiting for you on the other side of this or you're not likely to have the level of dedication you need to have.

For now, though, we're going to talk about what it means to be an expert. The definition you have in your mind of what an expert is, is a result of the experts you've known and the things you've been told about expertise. Much of what you've been told isn't true at all.

Consider the experts you know in your life— particularly those who are experts in the area you're interested in. What makes them an expert? If you can, research to figure out the journey of those experts you admire. Success leaves clues, and you'll probably be surprised by what you find. You'll probably find that there isn't anything really different or special about these experts. They are people, just like you, who became dedicated to their topic, just like you can.

If you have a little voice in your head right now that's telling you that you can't do this, that you can't become an expert, it's time to quiet that voice. My goal is to inspire you and give you the tools you need to succeed. Loosen up your mind and let go of what you previously thought about expertise.

Experts Know More about Their Topic than Most

Now that you've looked to the experts you've admired and thought about their journeys, break things down a little more and consider why you perceive these people to be experts. What is it about them? Do they teach others about the topic? Have they published on the topic? Do they offer coaching, consulting, courses, or mentorship? Do they have an online presence?

Break it down like this. If you peek behind the curtain, it will probably become pretty clear that most people are perceived as experts simply because they've declared that they are an expert. They've put themselves out there in some way that makes it clear they know what they are talking about. They invent, innovate, and keep up with the latest news and trends.

It will probably also become very clear that there are different levels of expertise. There's a certain mastery among the top experts in any field. Those are the people who seem to have an expertise that is unattainable. But there are bound to be experts who are newer to the topic. These experts may not have as much experience or as much exposure. They just know more about the topic than the average person and have declared their expertise in some way.

Experts Innovate

I mentioned this above, but I really want to highlight it. Generally, experts don't just know a lot about the topic. They are thought leaders. People turn to them because they know a lot about the topic and can demonstrate that.

Experts also innovate. They try new things others are afraid to try or don't know enough about the topic to even come up with. Experts find new ways to do things, invent things, and think about things in whole new ways.

They don't just fill their mind with information about the topic. They practice and invent and innovate. It's through this steady practice and by making mistakes and having successes that true expertise is born.

Experts Are Who Others Turn to For Advice

There are plenty of experts who just keep to themselves. I'm going to guess that that's not the type of expert you intend on becoming. You want to be an expert other turn to for advice. You want to be the first-person people think of when they want to learn more about a topic.

Consider the experts you turn to first. They put themselves out there. If they say something is true, others tend to believe them. They are the teachers and the leaders.

There are certainly some experts you're more attracted to than others. Just because someone is an expert doesn't mean you're ready to turn to them for advice. Not every expert is for everyone.

As you start to think about acquiring your own expertise, consider who your ideal audience is. How can you become the person they turn to first for advice? Emulate those you personally turn to.

Remember that people look up to experts. It doesn't matter if they're the top expert in the world or not. As long as the expert is helpful, knowledgeable, and well-practiced, they tend to get the respect of those in their audience. That's exactly what you're aiming for.

Teachers, Coaches, Mentors, and Consultants

There are certainly some experts who choose to keep to themselves. They might even go unknown as an expert, despite the fact that they know just as much, if not more, than any other expert out there.

I'll assume that you don't want to be an undercover expert. You have a goal in mind (that we'll get to the bottom of, shortly).

Maybe you want to become an expert to start or grow a business.

Maybe you want to become an expert to improve your job prospects.

Maybe you want to become an expert for personal fulfillment or to help people in some important way.

Maybe you want to become an expert in order to establish authority, which you'll be able to monetize in some way at some point in time (writing books, coaching, etc.).

That's exactly why so many experts also become teachers, coaches, mentors, consultants, and authors. Experts, in many different fields, tend to want to share their expertise with others. Often, teaching and sharing information and helping in other ways is the best way to display your expertise.

Remember— expertise is a moving target. There is no one definition of what an expert is or isn't. So, a lot of this comes down to *perceived* expertise. You don't just want to know a lot about your topic, you want to be thought of an expert. That's the best way to share what you know and get other benefits.

Consider the teachers, coaches, and mentors you have in your life. Think about the books you've bought on the topics that are important to you. You turn to those people for a reason. They are an expert in your eyes.

Does it matter if the author of the book you just bought only has a year or two of experience being an expert, if their information and experience helps you? Of course, it doesn't matter— as long as you learned something and what you learned was valid and valuable, that person was indeed the right expert for you at the time.

Becoming an Expert Will Serve You for a Lifetime

Whatever your goals are, becoming an expert in your field will serve you well for a lifetime. As an expert, you'll have doors opened for you that never would have been open before.

Becoming an expert is a means to an end. There's something you want to accomplish and you're reading this right now because you have a strong feeling that your expertise would make your goals possible.

If you start today, you can quickly become an expert in your chosen field. This isn't something with an endpoint. You'll continue reading, researching, practicing, experimenting, and sharing throughout your life.

You'll become more of an expert over time as you achieve mastery. In the meantime, you're going to easily achieve a level of expertise that can serve you very well now and, in the future, — in as little as 30 days.

Being perceived as an expert instantly puts you above the rest. You'll be able to create your own opportunities and choose your own path throughout life. You'll be able to achieve your goals and help other people as well.

You might wish you could just snap your fingers and learn everything you need to know. There's no getting around it— it's a process. You need to be okay with starting small today and working your way up. You won't have the same expertise in 30 days as someone who's been practicing something for 10 years. But, with some smart methods and tools, you can get pretty darn close, depending on the topic.

Buckle up— you're in for a wild lifelong ride.

Experts Never Stop Learning and Growing

Let's talk a little more about this journey. You aren't going to read a book or even 10 books on your topic and decide that you're "done" learning how to be an expert. Yes, you can achieve a certain level of expertise pretty much right away. You can be perceived as an expert as long as you know more than the people in your audience.

But you have to keep going. You have to get it in your mind right now that there's no endpoint. You'll be studying your topic and learning and growing for the rest of your life. You're going to be a thought leader and a true expert in your niche. That means keeping up with the changes and innovating within your niche.

I'd go as far as to say that the true mark of someone who is *not* an expert is that they think they know it all. A true expert knows that there is no way to know it all. A true expert knows what they don't know.

If someone, even an expert you currently look up to, tries to tell you that they know everything and that they have all the answers, it's time to be skeptical of them. A true expert sometimes doesn't have all the answers. They know that there are others out there who know more about a specific sub-topic of expertise than they do. A true expert looks forward to practicing things and making mistakes. A true expert is okay with telling you that they will research a certain question and get back to you with an answer, because they know where and how to do the research.

That's what you need to do. You'll quickly gain the respect of your audience if you're very honest and upfront in everything you do. There's no need to put on a front and 'fake it until you make it.' You need to put your all into developing your expertise so you can do a service to yourself and your audience.

Prepare yourself for a lifetime of learning. Ideally, you should love your topic. There should be a passion there that drives you to keep learning. You probably won't be able to become a top expert in a topic you don't care that much about. If your motivations and drive aren't in the right place, you might start off okay but quickly lose interest.

I think that's why there are so few true experts out there. Many people are afraid to follow their passions and achieve their goals as a result of following their passions. People often chase expertise for the wrong reasons. They see the money, fame, and respect others are getting and want that for themselves. The trouble is that they weren't really ever in tune with that topic. They didn't have the right goals and motivations.

If you can focus on a topic that you are passionate about and marry that with the goals you have for your life, business, work, family, and everything else, you'll probably be very successful. You'll be motivated to push through even when the going gets tough.

You've no doubt heard the expression that success doesn't happen in a straight line. You have one plan for your life. You plan to become an expert in your field and achieve all of your goals. But you have to know that you're going to have a lot of ups and downs along the way.

Sometimes, you will lose steam for your topic. Sometimes, all the work will damper your passions somewhat. You need to be prepared for that and keep your eye on the prize.

Start small and work your way up. You can absolutely call yourself an expert on your chosen topic, and for many topics, you can do so within 30 days of avid study and dedication. The first month will be easy— it's keeping things going where it gets difficult.

Prepare yourself for the long haul, even as you're lured by the thought of becoming an expert in the quick and easy way, I'm going to show you. I could easily sell many more copies of this book if I promised that you could become an expert in a day or something like that. But, I'm most interested in helping you live the kind of life you want to live. That means, I'm going to help you reach those quick goals— I'm going to teach you amazing ways to become a true expert faster than you ever thought possible. But I'm also going to help prepare you for a lifetime of success.

Revisiting the Word "Expert"

Hopefully, some of your preconceived notions about what expertise means have been broken down. Next, we're going to talk a little more about the word and how to achieve it.

The word "expert" might mean something different to you than it does to the next person. Someone else might not consider someone an expert unless they have decades of experience under their belt. I think we can agree that that's faulty thinking— does someone who's been avidly studying a topic for 5 years have nothing to say?

If you've been avidly studying something for a month, reading books, frequently topical forums, working with an expert mentor, practicing, etc., do you have any insight to offer to the person who's just getting started?

I think you do. And I think it's perfectly reasonable to call yourself an expert if you have dedicated yourself and have something to offer to your audience. Are you more expert than a newbie? Can you smooth their path and help them? Can you answer their questions? Then, to them, you are an expert.

It's so important to keep it in your mind that there are different levels of expertise. Eventually, you want to reach the level of mastery. But you can easily reach those earlier levels very quickly— even within the month.

There's a fairly well-known concept many people think of when it comes to expertise. You can think of it on a scale from 1-10.

Level 1 would be the total beginner— someone who probably wouldn't be considered much of an expert, if at all. They know more than someone at a level 0, of course... but those people aren't interested in the topic.

Level 10 would be the top expert— a master of the topic. This would be the very best of the best. This is the level you would strive to reach, someday. You would never reach it in a few hours or even a few years. This would be part of your lifelong journey.

You probably fall somewhere in the middle. At the end of the jumpstart 30-day journey you're going to take, you'll fall even higher on the scale.

A level 5 can mentor a level 1, right? A level 2 or a 3 could mentor a level 1, but the level 1 student would quickly catch up to the level 2 or 3 mentor.

This scale can really help you wrap your mind around what expertise really is. It's no good to be an expert in a vacuum. You're probably not interested in becoming an expert just for your own edification. You're interested in becoming an expert so you can help people, further your life, business, career, or whatever it is you've set your sights on.

Should you wait until you're an expert level 8, 9, or 10 before you start going after your goals? Definitely not. You can start right away. Dedicate yourself to this. If you work it, you can truly become an expert, and quickly.

You'll be doing yourself and your audience a disservice if you wait. There are people who there who need and want your help. You have goals that you've been sitting on for way too long. Now's the time to really go after them.

In fact, you'll be doing yourself a disservice also if you wait. When you're at the lower levels, and trying to help others, you'll be asked questions that you won't know the answers to. Finding the answers will move you up the ladder quicker than any other means.

It's Easier than You Think to Become an Expert

I hope you're feeling really motivated at this point. You're pumped up and ready to start in on your journey to become an expert. You know that becoming an expert is a means to an end. You have huge goals and dreams and you're going to stop at nothing to make them happen. Becoming a respected expert in your field is a fantastic way to achieve your goals and get to where you want to be.

If there's any takeaway I want to make sure you have down pat at this point, I want you to know that it doesn't take a lifetime to become an expert. You can become an expert, and you can start within the next 30 days, or possibly even sooner.

This is something you can truly start today. After you read this book, you can develop your plan and follow through. You'll work your way toward becoming an expert a little bit each day. Little by little, but faster than you think, you'll develop a workable level of expertise that will take you far.

In his book "Outliers," Malcolm Gladwell tells us that it takes 10,000 hours to become an expert. He believes you that you need to spend this time intentionally as you try to become an expert.

That book has been extremely popular. So popular that the "10,000" hours are often quoted as fact. I agree that it might take that long to reach a certain level of mastery. But I think that putting a specific hour limit on it might be too restrictive.

Remember— that level 5 expert has something to offer, even if he's not at a level 10 yet. That level 3 expert has something to offer, even if she's not at a level 5 yet.

I recommend that you not restrict yourself or discourage yourself in this way. Yes, you need to dedicate yourself and really focus on whatever it is you're determined to become an expert in. But you don't have to wait "10,000" hours to call yourself an expert. That's pretty short-sighted, especially when you have real goals that you want to achieve by showcasing your expertise.

Another author I admire, Jason Fladlien, has said that you can become an expert in 15 hours. His belief is that 15 hours of dedicated study, on any topic, will turn you into an expert. The thought is that you'll know more than most people after 15 hours of solid study.

He also believes that it will help you — a lot— if you put a specific hour figure on your path to becoming an expert. It's not the "15 hours" that's important, it's having an end-goal in mind.

It's hard to wrap your mind around a lifetime of dedicated study. That seems impossible to start... how do you even know where to start? When you're faced with a massive length of time like "10,000 hours" or "a lifetime," it's so daunting that you might give up altogether.

When you have an easy number like "15," you're a lot more likely to push through. 15 hours is doable, right? It absolutely is. There's an easy end there, something you can achieve.

Do I believe you can become an expert in 15 hours? Yes, I do. It depends on the topic. It depends on how you define "expert." It also depends on your goals and how you go about achieving those goals.

But someone who really dedicates 15 hours of study is going to know more than the person who's dedicated 1 or 0.

Is that the endpoint? No. It's a start, if anything. But, it's a solid start and it's more than the average person does. As long as you know more than the average person in your audience, you can consider yourself to be an expert.

My own philosophy falls somewhere in between. I do think it helps to have an endpoint as you start on your path to becoming an expert. It's not a true endpoint, as this is a lifelong journey. You will eventually achieve your 10,000 hours. You will eventually achieve that master level... if you want to, and if you spend years and years becoming an expert in just one field.

In Jason's case, I know him well, and I know that he loves to acquire expertise in dozens and dozens of different fields, and spending shorter time on each subject, so that he can talk and write with confidence, is what he's going after. He can create an info product about a topic where he has studied hard, and that info product will be helpful to all the many people that haven't spent the 15 hours or whatever amount of time Jason (or you or I) have spent.

In my eyes, that is a perfectly acceptable level of expertise, and what we write about or teach or talk about after that short amount of time will benefit our audience, who don't want to spend those 15 hours because they have better things to do with their time.

I'm going to have you start your journey over the next 30 days. I want you to dedicate yourself to becoming an expert over the next month. Can you achieve a 2, 3, 4, or a 5 on the "expert" scale by that time? I think you probably can.

30 days is do-able. It's easier than you think to become an expert; you just need a mindset shift.

You have to be willing to dedicate yourself to do it. You have to follow through and do a little bit every day. Spend an hour or more every day on this, for 30 days. You can do that, right? You need to really focus on this and develop a game plan that you can follow.

You have to be willing to acquire the knowledge you need. You have to be willing to read, look things up, come up with your own questions, interact with others, and possibly hire a mentor or coach. Those things can all help you over the next 30 days, and beyond.

If you want to succeed, you need to have a plan, goals, and the drive to follow through. You aren't going to become an expert through osmosis. You aren't going to become an expert just by deciding that you want to be one. You become an expert through study and practice.

It's fine to decide that you want to become an expert. But you have to know why. Why do you want to become an expert? Why is it so important to you that you're reading this right now? What is it that you really want to achieve?

What are your goals? We've talked about possibilities for life, business, work, and more. Sit down and brainstorm what it is you really want to achieve. Maybe you think it will help you achieve more money and get more recognition. But those things are an end-goal. Do you want an easier life? Do you want to live life on your own terms? What is your WHY for wanting to become an expert?

You also have to have the passion and drive to follow through. It's easy to decide you want to do something in the beginning. Maybe there is an expert you admire, and you really want to emulate that person. That's not enough to carry you through to the end. You can't just decide that you want to do this without feeling that drive and passion.

If you want to achieve true expertise, then you need to push yourself. You need to feel like nothing is going to stop you. You should really feel immersed in the journey you're about to embark on. If you don't feel that way or if you're not sure, it's time to do some more soul-searching.

Next, we'll go deeper into why you want to become an expert and the purpose it will serve for you.

Your Purpose for Becoming an Expert

You need a purpose. As we've talked about already, you can't just decide to become an expert for no reason.

The dedication and follow-through are what sets true experts apart from everyone else. Those who will never follow through will never achieve a level where they can consider themselves to be an "expert." Those people might try to take the easy way out— to "fake it until they make it."

That's not what you want to do, of course. This is a journey you're excited to be on. You know that becoming an expert is going to change your life in incredible ways. This is a decision that's going to serve you extremely well in more ways than one.

You need to have your purpose at the top of your mind.

Are you in this because it will help you start or further your business? Experts are often paid more highly than others. Experts know all the ins and outs of a topic and stand out in the competition. Your expertise can help open doors for you to earn more money and make more of an impact in your space.

Are you in this because you want to further your career? Experts are promoted and given better positions than those who haven't achieved a certain level of expertise. If you want to promote, make more money, and get more respect in the workplace, then you really have to work on what you know and how you present yourself.

Do you want to become an expert to help people? Experts can really give back to other people. You can use your expertise to help make life better or easier for other people.

Do you want to become an expert to change something in your life? It may be that you have certain hobbies, goals, and aspirations that you can't make work until you are an expert.

What is your purpose? What's going to drive you?

Becoming an expert can better your business or improve your value in the workplace. Becoming an expert can help you help yourself and others. What do you really hope will come from this?

You need to figure out your short-term goals. Your first short term expert plan will take place over the next 30 days— I'm going to tell you exactly what you need to know. What do you want to have achieved over the next 30 days? What level of expertise do you want to have reached?

You also need to figure out your long-term goals. What do you want to achieve over the next year, 5 years, 10 years, and more? How will becoming an expert on your topic help you?

Or is becoming an expert in a particular area just something that you want for now, and not to make a lifelong crusade? That's OK, it might be something you want to develop expertise on for the purpose of writing a book or creating a product or teaching a course and then you might not need to go any further. Some people become "temporary" experts on single subjects, and then move on to other skills that they wish to master. Is that what you want, or do you want to evolve your expertise about a single subject for the long term?

Determine how developing your expertise fits into this and come up with a plan. You need to know what you're aiming for and exactly how you're going to get there.

Will you read on your topic every day? Will you study under another expert? Brainstorm your plans, now.

Do you want to sell in the field? Do you want to start or grow a business? Do you want people to hire you as a teacher, coach, or mentor? Do you want to consult or speak? What is it, very specifically, that you want to gain from being an expert?

As an expert, you want to get more out of life. You've asked and answered a lot of questions about your plans at this point. It's all designed to help you get the best possible start. Go out there and make it happen!

Please don't just skim over this section. Really think on it and write your reflections down. It's important to write your goals down and revisit them on a regular basis. If you know why you're doing this, you'll be a lot more likely to follow through.

If you don't have a well thought out purpose for becoming an expert, then you probably won't follow through. If you have a well thought out purpose and a solid set of specific goals, then you probably will follow through and succeed. I know which option is more appealing to me— now it's your turn.

What Will You Become an Expert On?

Now, it's time for you to choose the exact topic you want to become an expert in. You may have it in mind already. Even if you do, it's important to do some fine-tuning. For example, the narrower your topic, the easier it will be to achieve expertise and recognition.

If your topic is very broad, then there's really no way to go deep there. For instance, if you decide to become an expert on weight loss, what does that really mean? You can try to achieve expertise on the topic of weight loss, but there's just so much there.

It's much easier to become an expert on a particular area of weight loss. For example, if you're passionate about the Paleo Diet, you can become an expert on that. It's much easier to study that narrow area of health and weight loss than it is to target weight loss as a whole.

If you're passionate about helping authors write and publish books, you might be tempted to go full steam ahead and become an expert on the topic yourself. But, it's easier to become an expert in a narrower way, at least at first. You can become an expert on helping romance fiction authors self-publish books on Amazon Kindle, for instance.

When people think of expertise, they often think too broad. Really, it might serve you and your audience better if you narrow things down. Be more specific. Focus, and you can more easily achieve expertise and reach an audience much more easily.

After you've developed expertise on a narrow subject, then you can begin to go broader, but before going broader I would recommend you go deeper in your narrow topic.

What to Do If You Already Know What You Want to Become an Expert On

If you already know what you're interested in becoming an expert on, break it down. Really turn the topic over and think about your goals. Do you need to know absolutely everything about the more general topic, or would it serve you better to specialize? Seek out other experts and see how they handle it. After you've achieved expertise and mastery in one area, you can certainly branch out wider in your field.

What to Do If You Don't Have Any Ideas for Your Expertise

It's most likely the case that you know exactly what you want to become an expert on, or you at least have a vague idea. If you don't, though, the options can be overwhelming.

Again, it all comes back to figuring out your goals. Why are you doing this and what do you want to achieve? Once you know that, you can examine the broad topics and specific topics and choose something you'd like to focus on.

Depending on your goals, there are some things you'll want to consider. First, are you passionate about the topic? If you're not driven and passionate, you're probably not going to follow through in the long term. Examine the passionate before you choose your topic.

Which blogs do you visit every day? Which non-fiction books do you already read for pleasure? Which experts do you admire and hope to emulate? This can help you determine what you should choose.

You should also examine your goals. It might be that your top passion doesn't line up with your goals, exactly. Maybe becoming an expert on topic X wouldn't serve you but becoming an expert on topic Y will. Or maybe becoming an expert on topic X will open up the doors for you to move to topic Y later, whereas you can't see yourself just diving into topic Y instantly.

I'll assume that most people want to become an expert because they want to earn more money, further their life in some way, or help people in some way. Make sure the topic you choose serves that purpose. You can become an expert on basket weaving, but does that really help you reach your goals? Are there really opportunities to share your expertise there? Find something that ticks all the boxes.

Choosing Your Topic

Now it's time to choose your topic, or to narrow your topic down if you already have one in mind. Your topic is extremely important. If you focus on something that won't help you achieve your goals, you've essentially wasted your time. If you focus on something that doesn't have a large and interested audience, your plans may be dead in the water.

Most people want to become an expert in something to further their life and business in some way. You don't want to know something just to know it— it's really a means to an end. Really think long and hard about your goals and about how your chosen topic will help you reach your goals.

It may be the case that your topic is fairly pre-determined. If your plan is to further your career in some way, consider which specialty you can focus on within the wider topic. What would be most impressive to those in-the-know? Which focus will help you keep up with the 'big dogs' or stand out from the crowd? Remember not to choose something just to choose it, choose something because it will help you get to where you want to be.

If you want to start a business, in either the online or offline world, you might be at a total loss for choosing your topic. You know that there are plenty of opportunities out there for you to earn a fantastic income and build your dream life by owning your own business. Where should you start?

Only you know the reasons you're interested in becoming an expert on something. No matter what your exact reason is, you have to know how to choose your general topic as well as your more specific topic.

Again, start with what you're passionate about. You're going to be spending a lot of time with this topic, so it has to be something you'll really enjoy. The lure of the money you can earn with a particular topic might be really strong, but is it strong enough to keep you going?

Passion isn't enough, of course. You also have to make sure the potential is there with your topic. Are there enough people interested in the topic? Will you be able to achieve your goals, financial or otherwise, with a focus on the topic?

It's also really helpful to sort of study how current experts on the topic are faring. How did those experts get to where they are today? Are they where you want to be as far as recognition and the impact they make on the audience? How about financially?

You have to know that the topic you want to choose is going to smooth the way for you to reach your goals. If there's no audience, no money, and no possibilities, then it's not the topic for you.

What to Do If You're Totally Stuck for Ideas

If you're totally stuck for topic ideas and you've gone through your passions, it's time to do some more digging. You can search online to start to spark some ideas. Browsing the non-fiction section at Amazon is a great way to start. There are a ton of different topic ideas— you can also get a feel for who the top experts are in each field. Experts tend to publish books to spread their ideas.

You can also search for the top blogs on topics you're interested in. These days, many people turn to the online world for the information and insight they need. These bloggers are the go-to experts for a wide audience. Look at what they blog about and which topics get the most activity and commentary. Those might be sub-topics you can dive into.

You really have to work your way backward. You have to know what you want and why you want to become an expert.

Take some time to brainstorm and figure this out. Remember that it's better if you specialize. When you specialize, you can develop your expertise much more quickly. It's so much easier to have a narrow focus. There's less information to absorb and you do a better job with the information you do absorb.

It's also a lot easier to make a splash when you go narrow (and deep) with a topic. There are probably fewer experts on the playing field. If your goal is to break through and be seen as an expert quickly, this may be the way to go for you.

Moving Forward with Your Topic

You don't want to rush this decision. At the same time, it's often not as difficult as some people make it out to be. Don't kid yourself— if you're stewing over this decision for days, weeks, months, or even years, there's probably something else that's holding you back. It might be that you're scared to move forward. What if you fail? What if you don't like the topic after all?

But remember, if you don't move forward, time will anyway. If you've been delaying (a.k.a. procrastinating) for months or years, take stock of the situation, think where you would be now if you started those months or years ago, and how things would be different... then don't repeat the procrastination again, or start it in the first place.

You need to approach this logically. Is this topic going to help you achieve whatever it is you want to achieve? Is it narrow enough that you can quickly achieve expertise and become highly regarded for the audience? If it is, and you're sure it suits your path, then you need to go with it.

By the way, most people aren't experts on just one topic. Just because you choose this topic today doesn't mean you can't become an expert on an additional topic in the future. You're probably already an expert on more than one topic (whether or not your current expertise suits your goals is another story).

Don't take that as encouragement to skip around from topic to topic. If you want to succeed and become an expert, then you need to focus. Are you willing to dedicate yourself to this and really focus? It's time to make it happen.

Gathering the Knowledge, You Need

Now that you've chosen your topic and you're dedicated to this, it's time to gather the knowledge you need. You're going to become an expert— that means you need to study hard.

In these early days, you're going to really be working. The honest fact is that you won't become an expert if you don't study and learn.

Expertise isn't just like going to school. In school, you were forced to learn a variety of topics that you probably couldn't have cared less about.

Now, you get to choose. You get to choose to really focus on something you're passionate about. Not only are you passionate about it, but it's also something that's going to help you change your life. That's very exciting!

It's important to think about how you learn best. Do you learn best by reading books? Do you learn best by attending classes or seminars in person? Do you learn best by working with other learners? Do you learn best by watching or practicing? Do you learn best by finding mentors (mentors can be people who don't even know that they're your mentor) and following them, doing what they do, etc.

Studying and learning doesn't have to be dull. You can choose exactly the method that appeals to you the most. If you like to read, then you can acquire your expertise by reading. If you learn better by practicing, you can acquire your expertise through practice.

Most people, of course, learn best through a mixture of all the different methods. The important thing is that you immerse yourself in what you're doing. Every day, you need to do something that contributes to your journey to become an expert.

I'm not saying you have to spend hours and hours of dedicated study each day. There are many other things going on in your life and you can only fit so much in. It's that all-or-nothing attitude that stops people before they even get started.

It certainly doesn't have to be all-or-nothing! You'll almost definitely burn out if you approach this with that attitude.

Instead, I'd like you to cut yourself a break. It's time to use the 'slow and steady wins the race' method. You're going to focus on your study a little bit each day. You won't beat yourself up if you miss a day— but you will make a concentrated effort to make it happen.

Every day, you're going to do something. Whether it's read a book, listen to a seminar, attend a class, chat with a mastermind group or coach, or something else. Ideally, you'll spend one or more hours on expert study every day.

Setting Yourself Up for Success

There are so many things you can do to help ensure you're successful. First, you have to realize that right now, you're probably feeling more passionate and excited than you will for the entire next month. There are going to be times when you don't feel like studying and learning and applying yourself to become an expert.

You have to plan for those ups and downs. You'll want to skip the study sometimes. What are you going to do to make it easier for yourself? It's time to start planning ahead.

This can be as simple as finding and subscribing to blogs and Facebook groups or Google+ communities that talk about your topic of interest or setting up Google Alerts for the main keywords that you've chosen to become an expert about. There are bound to be popular blogs out there that you can read on a regular basis. These blogs will probably have a lot of helpful background information on your topic, including facts and opinion. Best of all, as is important for any expert, you'll also have access to all the latest and greatest information on your topic.

We'll talk a lot more about this a bit further on, but blogs and groups are also a nice way to interact with the people of your audience. You can observe the comments section to see what kinds of questions people ask other experts. You can even jump in, even when it's not your own blog or group, to help answer questions yourself. This is how you start to be seen as an expert and authority on your topic. Start interacting and start teaching, even at this early stage. Blogs and groups are a fantastic resource for anyone on an expert journey, so I highly recommend you make use of them.

You probably won't remember to visit these blogs and groups on your own, though. You might get busy and it will slip by the wayside. You need to subscribe to them, so they land in your inbox every time there is an update. This is a big part of setting yourself up for success. Make things easy for yourself and automate whenever you can.

It will be hard to remember to do things, like visit new blogs, when you're first getting started. That's because doing these things isn't yet a habit of yours. Soon enough, it will become a habit for you to take part in daily learning. For now, automate.

You might even enlist the help of a friend or even an accountability partner to help you keep going. If you have a friend who has similar goals and is studying the same thing, it's a lot easier for you to keep going yourself. There's more of a commitment there. It's easier to let yourself down than it is to let other people down. Joining a mastermind group is a fantastic first step.

In addition to reading blogs and groups and subscribing to them, you are going to need to find great books to read on the topic. Beyond that, though, you may want to see if there are any courses you can take related to the topic. Courses are a fantastic way to set yourself up for success. They are generally much more costly than a single book, which makes you more likely to follow through with them.

There may be online courses or courses offered in a traditional classroom setting. Wherever you take them, these courses can help you absorb more information more quickly and help you keep your commitment since you'll be required to keep up with the teacher, other attendees, and the material.

That's not to say that coursework is more valuable than reading on your own. Sometimes people find that structured courses just don't move at the speed they prefer. There's nothing wrong with finding your own reading material and zooming through it at your own speed. If you're dedicated and you're ready to immerse yourself, you can make fantastic headway, very quickly, when it comes to learning your topic.

More on Reading Books

If you haven't gathered it already, you're going to be doing a lot of reading on your path to becoming an expert. There really isn't any way around that, for most topics. This isn't an issue for you if you're someone who enjoys reading. If you don't enjoy reading, then you're probably dreading this. How are you going to commit to something like this if you don't like the task of reading?

Honestly, if you really enjoy your topic, then you'll probably find that reading about your topic is enjoyable. If you enjoy your topic and you are determined to reach your goals, you will probably feel driven to read these books. It won't feel like work or a chore— it will be something you look forward to.

But, for argument's sake, let's say that you absolutely, positively despise the idea of reading books on your topic. Don't give up. Don't let that fear or hatred of reading cause you to turn your back on your goal of becoming an expert on your topic. There are so many other options out there for you.

First of all, you're probably well aware of YouTube. There are bound to be tons of high-quality videos, on YouTube and elsewhere, on your topic. Look them up and watch them. You'll learn a lot. This is even a good thing to do if you do love to read— learning in multiple ways helps give you a more well-rounded experience.

You can also search for podcasts on your topics. There are many experts who run regular podcasts that you can download or listen to. This is a great option, because you can download the episodes to your phone, iPad, computer, or whatever device you prefer to listen on. You can listen while in the car, cleaning the house, or while you're doing just about anything. Remember— you're trying to make it easy on yourself, and podcasts are a great easy learning tool.

Eventually, the goal would be for you to have your own YouTube channel, podcast, and books. You'll release whatever type of content suits you the best, of course. And we'll discuss why it's important to spread content of all types far and wide when you're trying to brand yourself as an expert.

While you're in this active, hardcore learning stage, you need to find all different kinds of content in many different formats to learn from. Whether you mostly prefer to listen, or watch, or read, set yourself up right now while you're really excited about this journey. Get all of your learning material lined up.

Every day, schedule in some time for yourself to go through it. Read a little each day, listen to a podcast in the car, and watch a short YouTube video on your lunch break. Little by little, piece by piece, you'll have expert-level knowledge on your topic.

In these early days, you might want to schedule in more time than you would normally. Instead of watching TV at night, immerse yourself with your study materials. Make sure your family knows your intention and why you're on this journey. Have them help point you to new materials they see out and about— they'll naturally do that, once they know you're really interested in a topic.

Don't Just Read— Practice

You can't just read and study all the time. If you want to become an expert quickly, then you have to put what you learn into practice. What that means varies depending on your area of interest.

For example, you might be studying a topic that lends itself very well to practice and application. In some fields, that's really the only way to truly learn. In that case, the practice part of things would make up the bulk of your learning.

But you just might have to create your own opportunities for practice and application if you're not sure. For instance, if your plan is to become an expert in business, you might run and publish your own case studies as a way of applying what you learn. Publish your case studies on a blog so other people can follow. This method kills two birds with one stone— you'll be getting traffic and you'll be practicing what you learn.

Sometimes, it's a lot easier to learn the material than it is to try it. It's a lot less intimidating, too. When you put something into practice, you might make mistakes, right? That's a scary thought.

You can't just be a "book learner," though. If you want to be a true expect, then you need to try things out. You have to be willing to make errors and fix them and learn the ins and outs of everything you're trying to learn. If you do that, if you make that effort, then you'll be many steps ahead of most so-called experts out there.

I can't tell you specifically what you need to do to practice what you're learning. The exact steps vary greatly depending on what it is you're trying to learn at the expert level. It might be as simple as blogging about your journey. It might be that you need to test things out in a lab. It might be that you need to study under someone who is living your topic every day in their job.

Figure out what you need to do to get some hands-on time with your topic. Ideally, you'll get some study and research time and hands-on practice time every day. Even if you only get a little bit of time each day with your topic, the daily effort will really pay off for you.

It's immersing yourself in your topic and really being aware of the time you spend with your topic that makes a difference. You need to create a schedule for yourself and stick to it. On top of it all, you need to keep your goals in mind. That will help you stay motivated. If you know what you're aiming for, you'll be a lot more likely to get it.

Start Writing about What You're Learning

I've found that one of the best ways to grow and share my expertise is to write about my topic. There's something about putting pen to paper or fingers to keyboard that helps to cement the information. Writing about your topic helps you think critically about what you're learning. It makes it more real— more concrete.

As you write, questions enter your own mind about what you're writing about. You start to notice that there are gaps that you think a reader will notice, and you then start to fill in the gaps not only in what you're writing, but also in your own knowledge about the topic. If you're writing something shorter, like a blog post, then people will post comments with questions, and you'll realize what you've omitted or haven't explained well. And so, it goes, incremental steps further along on your path to becoming an authority.

There are two benefits here. You'll more readily absorb and truly learn the information. This is a huge benefit to you. If you write a little each day you can very quickly become an expert. You'll read, study, practice, and share what you know. That's what experts do.

Your writing will also help you build up your reputation as an expert. There are people out there who are ready and willing to learn from you. When you explore and share what you know with the written word, people will come to see you in a whole new way. They'll start to think of you as an expert. So, by writing, you'll be helping yourself and helping others and building up a reputation as an expert that will serve you well for a lifetime.

You might be wondering which format your writing should take. That really depends, and I actually recommend you write in more than one format, depending on the purpose.

When you're first learning and exploring and you're very new, you'll probably write more for yourself. You can keep a journal of your observations and experiences— of your ups and your downs. This journal will help to cement the information in your mind. It will help you form your own opinions and really reflect on everything you're doing.

Keeping a journey is extremely helpful. Many experts journal their thoughts and experiences regularly, even when they're well into the expert stage. They help show your growth and allow for a lot of reflection about yourself and your topic. There's a lot of freedom in this kind of writing since it's not for anyone but yourself. You can really open up and explore freely, when you might hold back if you were writing for an audience.

You can also write for others in a variety of formats. It's a great way to showcase your expertise and make a name for yourself. Remember— it's one thing to know your stuff as a true expert, but it's another thing altogether to become perceived as an expert by others. I'm assuming that your goals relate, at least partially, to becoming perceived as an expert. In that case, writing and putting out content is one of the best ways to establish yourself.

You can write blog posts, as I mentioned earlier on. Put it in your mind that you're going to create an authority blog on your topic. You eventually want your blog to be a place where people go to learn more, interact with one another, consult with you as an expert, and keep up with the latest news on the topic.

You can study current authority blogs to get a feel for what you should be doing. There's a right way to blog and a wrong way to blog. Make sure you focus your blog specifically on your topic and make sure there's an audience for whatever it is you want to write about. What is unique about your insights or way of thinking? There has to be a reason people are going to read your blog on a regular basis. Figure out what makes you unique in a crowded field of experts, and your blog writing might become more popular than you imagine, in a much shorter period of time.

You might also consider writing and releasing your own books. I really enjoy writing books on a variety of topics. It's exciting, fun, and profitable. I get to share great information with my audience. Writing also helps me think about all different angles of any given topic. Writing books in my areas of expertise has been a very valuable exercise.

Whether you're writing for yourself or to help educate others, I encourage you to make writing part of your expert-building strategy. You'll be able to get to where you want to be much more quickly. Don't just read, study, and practice— write and teach. You'll be a more well-rounded expert as a result.

Trying and Doing

How can you try and do what you're learning? As an expert, you're going to know enough to carve your own path. You're going to know enough to try different things out. That might mean experimenting, inventing, or performing your own case studies. What happens if you do this? What happens if you do that?

People will be looking up to you as an expert. In most cases, they expect that you won't just regurgitate known information; they also expect that you will innovate and create in your field. If you don't feel ready to do that yet, don't worry. With solid study and practice time, you will be ready. In fact, it will become like second nature to you to create in this way.

You have to be a leader, though. You can't just expect opportunities to fall into your lap. As an expert, you're going to be creating your own opportunities. Other people are going to follow your lead. It's a magnificent thing, when you get to that point— you just have to put in the work to get there.

Interact with Other Experts

One of the best ways to further your own expertise is to interact alongside other experts. In fact, I'd go as far as to say that you should avoid people who are dashing your dreams and ideas. Instead, surround yourself with those who have similar goals or who have already achieved those goals. You need to immerse yourself in success, rather than doubt.

Other experts have gone through their own journey. It's important to have a well-rounded view of your area of expertise. Really, the only way to gain that is by surrounding yourself with other experts. You can learn from their journeys and the way they approach the topic.

You can join a mastermind team of likeminded thinkers. Masterminds are a fantastic tool, and you'll almost definitely see better results much more quickly on your journey to become an expert, if you join one. You'll surround yourself with people who are at various stages of their own journey. You'll get to bounce ideas around and learn from those who are on your level and above. You'll also learn a lot by helping those who are below your current level.

Where can you find these likeminded thinkers? Depending on your area of interest, there might be a regular club that meets in your area. You could even start your own, if there isn't anything going. Try searching Meetup.com to see if there are any great groups already running. You can also use that platform to easily connect with others online, for an offline meetup. There are bound to be others out there who want the same things you want.

You can also find likeminded thinkers online. There are tons of forums, both public and private, for just about every topic out there. You can easily find one of these forums to join. Start interacting with people— ask questions, answer questions, and bounce ideas around. Really get into the topic.

These days, you'll also be able to find likeminded thinkers via social media. There are plenty of social media groups out there— on Facebook, Google +, Twitter, and LinkedIn, depending on your topic. This is a great way to get to know people and interact with those who are interested in the same things you're interested in.

You can also find those who are already established as experts online and off. Figure out what they're doing and how they interact with their audience. Become part of their audience and have those experts become familiar with you. You should be networking and making connections everywhere you go.

You'll learn a lot along the way. If you visit topical forums and groups a little each day, and interact with top experts online a little each day, and meet in person with a mastermind group on a regular basis, and keep up with your studies and practice, you'll absolutely see results in an extremely short period of time. That's because you'll truly be immersing yourself in your topic.

This is how real results are achieved. It's not that you have to spend an enormous amount of time on your topic each day— you certainly don't. It's the concentrated effort. Just a little bit of time each day adds up to huge results when you look back over time. I'm going to have you start by focusing on the next 30 days— I think you'll be pleasantly surprised at what you achieve over that time.

Make Mistakes and Learn from Them

Another part of becoming a great expert is making mistakes and learning from them. If you haven't made mistakes related to your topic yet, then you probably aren't yet an expert! That's because true experts aren't afraid to try and fail at things. They know that they have to try new things in order to succeed.

You want to know more about your topic than just about anyone else, eventually, and you want to be perceived as an expert. You can't just 'play it safe' if that's your goal. You have to be willing to experiment, and test things out. You have to be willing to test and tweak your way to success.

If you're playing it safe all the time, you're really just staying on the surface of your topic. If you haven't made any mistakes, then you aren't practicing what you're studying. It's time to embrace mistakes because they are a very important part of the learning process.

I've made a ton of mistakes in marketing and business. But that's a huge part of the reason for my success. If I hadn't made those mistakes, I wouldn't be where I am today. I also wouldn't be as helpful in mentoring people. I can help them avoid mistakes and help them achieve their goals much more quickly. I'm so much more effective because I've been willing to try and fail.

That's what you need to be willing to do on your journey. You have to be willing to try things no one else will try. It's not just about making mistakes, of course. You need to be very keenly aware of course correction. If you do make a mistake, you don't need to beat yourself up about it— you need to be able to analyze where things went wrong.

If everything's sailing along just perfectly for you right now, that's great. But it also means you've really just scratched the surface. It means you have so much further to go. It's time to really dive in there. Expect that you'll make mistakes and have setbacks. Also, chalk those things up as victories because they're helping you analyze your topic in a much more critical way.

The fact is that experts have made mistakes. Newbies haven't made mistakes. You want to join the team of the former, rather than the latter. Allow yourself to make mistakes and put yourself into situations where you probably will make mistakes. Your results will be that much sweeter.

Be Mindful of What You're Doing and Why

You have to be mindful of what you're doing and why. Why are you on this journey to become an expert? What do you really hope to gain from it? I know I've asked you to do a lot of self-reflection so far... but get ready, because I'm going to ask you to do even more.

That's because I'm not just giving you the advice you've probably received before— "read a lot about your topic and you'll be an expert." That's because I don't think that *truly* makes you an expert. I think you have to be mindful and reflective and immersive along the way, if you want true results.

It's one thing to go through the motions of becoming an expert, ticking all the boxes. It's another thing altogether to actually know what you're doing and be aware of what you're doing so it serves you on your path to expertise.

Revisit your goals daily, if not more frequently. I sometimes suggest to people that they create a mind movie or a vision board. Feature your goals and desires in picture or movie form so you get that visual connection.

You can also use visualization to help you along the way. Close your eyes and visualize yourself in the expert role. What are you doing? Who are you surrounding yourself with? As an expert, what breakthroughs are you making and who are you helping? We think of visualization as a visual thing but try to incorporate all of your senses in your vision. It's like a guided daydream, where you get to choose and imagine your ideal outcome.

You have to make it inevitable in your mind that you will succeed. Be mindful of your journey and don't be afraid to make tweaks here and there. Where you are today as an expert is very different than where you'll be in 30 days from now or 6 months from now, if you follow the plan, I'm setting out for you. Be mindful, reflective, and laser-focused on getting to where you want to be.

Other Experts Will Help You Get to Where You Want to Be Much More Quickly

We've already talked about the fact that you should be learning from experts you admire. Take every opportunity to surround yourself with them and learn from them, and you'll get to where you want to be much more quickly.

Now, let's talk more about the hows and the whys. How are you going to find top experts to work with? Why is this really necessary when there are so many learning materials out there that you could just go it alone?

Why

First, let's talk about the why. Yes, you can learn a lot on your own. In fact, you're going to learn a lot on your own. You really have to be a self-starter if you want to become an expert.

But, part of the reason you're reading this right now is because you want to reach your goals more quickly. You don't want it to take years to become an expert. You want to achieve expert status more quickly.

That's why you need to stand on the shoulders of giants. Work with others, learn from their mistakes and insights, and have them help you on your direct journey. You'll become an expert more quickly— working with other experts is a shortcut that helps you achieve your dreams more quickly.

You'll be learning from the best. You'll be learning what worked for them and what didn't work for them. They'll help you cut down on your own learning curve.

You want to do this as quickly and efficiently as you can, right? You want to be a well-rounded, top expert yourself. Working with other experts is the best way to do that— in combination with the other things you're doing, of course.

How

Now let's talk about how you go about finding yourself an expert to study under. It can seem impossible. After all, you figure that many experts are busy with other commitments and aren't exactly ready to take on an apprentice.

Actually, there are plenty that are.

There are many experts out there who offer their services as a coach or a mentor. If you can find a good one, I think you'll be extremely pleased with your results. They might work with you in person or even online. Some coaches are very hands-on, while others just check in every now and then. You need to evaluate what they are offering, after you evaluate their credentials, to see if they work on a timeline that suits you.

It's extremely important to make sure you don't get sucked into high-priced coaching with little results. In the business world, there are unfortunately "coaching floors" that are essentially a bait and switch. They promise that you'll get to work with the high-end marketing expert, but instead you get stuck with a "coach" who is just a minimum wage employee of that person.

You can get coaching for fantastic prices. You can get coaching for exorbitant prices. Usually, you do get what you pay for— but not always. Please be mindful of who you're hiring and what you can expect to achieve in return.

If you've been networking and interacting with experts online or off, put out the feelers for where you might get coaching. Many experts have their coaching and mentorship information right on their website. Look at their terms and see if it suits you. If it doesn't, it might be possible to propose a modification— you never know until you ask.

What if you aren't quite ready for a formal mentor or coach? You can still learn from the best. Does your ideal expert run their own forum or membership site? Join it. Do they run a social media group related to your topic online? Join that. Interact on these places and get to know the expert. Don't hesitate to ask questions.

Does your ideal expert offer in-person classes near you? Take them up on it. Do they run a Meetup group? Start attending.

Do they write a blog online and allow for a lot of reader participation? Become an active part of that audience.

Essentially, you're going to choose someone or multiple someones that you really look up to— that you idealize as an expert. This is someone you hope to become like as an expert. You're going to figure out where opportunities exist to work with them or under them. Then, you're going to take advantage of all the opportunities that exist.

Start searching— I think you'll be surprised and really excited about the opportunities you find.

Learn from the Best

Stand on the shoulders of giants. You want to learn from the best. Many of the best experts on your topic are out there, right now, providing opportunities for you to learn from them.

When you learn from the best, you cut down on your own learning curve. They'll give you insights you never would have found on your own.

Sometimes, they'll show you what you *don't* want to do. You shouldn't just learn from one person all the time— I want to make that clear. When you learn from a variety of experts, you'll be able to pull bits and pieces out of what you like from each of them.

Let me tell you a secret. When you get up close and personal with any expert, you'll start to see flaws. Even though you aren't yet as much of an "expert" as they are, you'll see holes in what they are doing. You'll probably see that life isn't always as rosy as you might think it is for these successful experts.

Don't let that discourage you. Let that show you that experts are human, too. Let that show you that there isn't really anything that's different or special about these experts. They've simply already put the time in. They've simply declared that they are an expert and have done things that encourages others to see them in that way.

Most of all let that show you that there is indeed room for you to jump into the topic area as an expert yourself, and quite possibly improve on those others out there.

Seek out the very best. Find experts that excite you with their ideas and words. Find experts that inspire you to stay the path until you achieve your goals. When you do that, you'll be a lot more likely to follow through and become an expert— and, you'll be able to succeed more quickly because they've already cleared the path for you.

Learn What Worked for Them and What Didn't

Two of the best takeaways you can get from any expert is what worked for them and what didn't. You want to cut down on your own learning curve.

Experience is a great teacher, but better yet is letting someone else's experience shorten the time it takes to do the teaching.

You want to make mistakes… but you don't want to make mistakes that are easily avoidable and that have been made by dozens of experts before you. You want to make mistakes because you're innovating and cutting a new path, not because you didn't pay attention to the mistakes that were made by other experts before you.

Learn what worked. Learn the tricks of the trade from people who've been there. By studying the journeys of other experts, you'll be able to pick out these pearls of wisdom that will help you in your own path.

Learn what didn't work. You don't want to waste your time. Use these experts to gain insights you wouldn't have on your own.

I can't stress enough that if you want to become an expert more quickly, then you should learn from people who are already established. It's like having a cheat-sheet.

Remember that it's not necessarily all about finding a coach or a mentor, you can gain a lot of insights about what works and doesn't work by surrounding yourself with other people who are on the expert journey, or who just are very interested in your topic. Join or form a mastermind, group, or club. Join several of them, if you have the time for it and want to immerse yourself.

You can learn a lot from other people. It would be silly to go this alone when there are so many people out there freely sharing what has worked for them and what hasn't worked for them.

What to Look for In Other Experts

I wish I didn't have to write this here, but it's very important that you protect yourself. There are people out there who really are one thing but will present themselves as another thing.

There are people out there who will offer coaching sessions, declaring themselves as an expert, but who really don't have the knowledge and experience to help you.

There are people in groups and masterminds who inflate their results and make assumptions that lead to incorrect advice and information— whether they mean for it to be or not.

You have to know what to look for in other experts. You can't always take people at face value. This journey is important to you— don't rush into anything or work with anyone until you've taken the time to evaluate whether they really have the knowledge and know-how to help you.

What is their reputation? Have others worked with them and gotten results? That's probably the best indicator right there. If others have worked with them and gotten results, and the person is transparent and willing to share, then it's probably just fine to look up to that person as an expert.

Reflect Along the Way

I promised there would be plenty of opportunity for reflection, so here's more about that. I believe it's important to reflect on the things you're doing and the things that are important to you. If you don't, you'll be missing a lot of opportunity for learning along the way. When you reflect on important things, you'll see new pathways that will help you succeed. You'll learn more about what worked and didn't work. With just a little bit of time spent in reflection on a regular basis (daily) you can see some fantastic results.

As part of your reflection time, I believe you should set milestones for yourself along the way. In addition to your daily reflection, these milestones can help you figure out where to change and where to grow. You can connect your milestones with the longer-term goals you've set for yourself.

You have goals that you plan to reach. Hopefully, you've set goals for the next 30 days, 6 months, and beyond. These goals should be solid and specific. But, how do you know you're going to achieve those goals? It shouldn't be a surprise at the end. You shouldn't just know that you're going to reach those goals— there should be no doubt in your mind.

You know you're going to reach those goals because you're able to reflect on your milestones. Let's say you have a goal you want to reach by the end of these 30 days. You might set milestone check-ins for the first week, the second week, and the third week. That way, you can look at how far you've come and what you need to do to achieve the fourth week.

Don't over-complicate things. You might just tell yourself that you want to achieve X by Sunday, as part of your 30-day goal. You want to achieve X by the Sunday after that. On those Sunday's, sit down and journal or simply reflect on what you've done or not done to achieve these milestones. This can really be whatever you want it to be. It's designed to help you "check in" on yourself you're able to stay on the course you set for yourself.

I suggest you brainstorm as a way of setting these milestones. Think about your 30-day goal or your 6-month goal. What are all the things you need to do to achieve those goals? Write down everything you can think of.

Now remember, you also should be reflecting and making a decision at the start as to what level of expertise you want to reach. There's no shame in deciding that you want to be "just enough" of an expert so that you can teach the topic to those who are below that level. On a scale of 1 to 10 with 10 being ultimate authority, you might be happy reaching a level of 5. That still will be enough of an expert to be successful, and you might be able to reach that level in just 30 days, or 60 days, if you really apply yourself.

Of course, if you're determined to be a real authority on your topic, you probably want to go far beyond the initial sprint of the first 30 days, and perhaps keep advancing for years or for life. So, your regular reflection will help you make those decisions and keep you on track.

When you're finished, create a timeline for yourself. Figure out what you need to have done each month, each week, and each day in order to achieve your goal. You want to become an expert— but what does that mean? What does that entail, for you and your topic, specifically? I think you'll find that this is an extremely valuable exercise.

Remember to use other successful experts as inspiration if you're stuck. Examine the journey they went on. Ask yourself what they had to accomplish, and by when. Since you get the benefit of learning from their successes and failures, you might be able to ramp up your timeline a bit. You can do it on warp-speed since you're going to pick and choose from what worked and what didn't. You have a big-time advantage.

Journal your experiences along the way. Do this in whatever form works for you. Maybe you'd like to get one of those hardcover executive notebooks to brainstorm, journal, and reflect. Or, maybe it's more in your nature to want something special to journal in— like a handcrafted leather journal.

The fact is that this is a special process. You should pat yourself on the back, already. You've set a goal that you're determined to reach. You are really dedicating yourself to becoming an expert on your topic. Treat yourself right and get yourself something special— you'll be able to look back on your journal or notebook later on and smile, because you've come so far. Actually, this journal will be extremely handy if you eventually plan on offering your own coaching or mentoring services on your topic of expertise.

Journaling and reflection are a great way to improve your process. If you just barrel straight ahead without pausing to reflect, you'll be making a huge mistake. It will take you a lot longer and your knowledge won't be as vast as it would be otherwise.

It can take a while to get into the habit of journaling and reflection, of course. Be mindful of it for the next month or so. Take just 5 minutes at first, if that's easiest for you. I promise— you'll love the results it brings you on your path to becoming an expert.

Always look for ways you can improve. Don't be content with the thought that it's going to take you X amount of time to become a "true" expert. It's time for you to break down barriers and accomplish things so quickly that people will wonder how in the world you did it.

Don't let anyone tell you that you can't become an expert quite quickly. By being mindful of your process, inventing your own path, and pausing for reflection, you'll be able to accomplish whatever it is you've set out to accomplish.

Develop Your Weekly Expertise Schedule

If you want to be successful, then you need to be pretty detailed with the schedule you plan to follow. You don't have to study and work hard every hour of every day. But you do need daily consistent effort. If you don't stay the course and work on your expertise every day, it's going to take you a lot longer and you'll probably fall short of your goals.

I'm all about making things easier and more possible for the average person. That means helping you figure out the best possible shortcuts so you can become a successful expert and achieve your goals. Trust me when I tell you that you'll have better results if you make a commitment to yourself to do a little each day.

My most popular book is 5 Bucks a Day. This details my philosophy for the business-minded of focusing on building up their business just $5 a day at a time. I've based this philosophy on the saying, "How do you eat an elephant? One bite at a time!"

You can't eat the elephant all at once— it won't work. You can't become an expert in a day— at least not a very well-rounded one. But you can do it little by little. Those day-by-day activities really add up, even if they only take place for a short time each day.

In high school or college, you may have fallen into the habit of trying to cram for a test all at once. You know that isn't ideal. You know that you might remember just enough information to past the test, but not to have a mastery of it.

Here, today, you're not trying to cram for a test, and you don't have to study or do anything that you don't like. That's the beauty of this! You get to choose your topic. You get to choose the topic that means the most to you and that you truly want to become an expert in.

There's no reason to 'cram for the test' because this is your life and you're now choosing the direction it goes in. It can be hard to break those old habits, though. Life can get busy and the activities you need to do to build to the expert level might fall by the wayside.

That's why you need to create an easy, bite-sized plan for yourself. When you have a daily plan where you only have to do a little bit at a time, it gets a lot less overwhelming for you. It gets pretty exciting, actually.

Getting Started with Your Plan

There's no one here to dictate your schedule— you only have to do what you want to do. So, now you get to decide. What do you need to do in order to become an expert? I've given you the pieces I suggest, right here in this book. Now, you just need to examine it, choose the parts that are right for you, and create a schedule for yourself. For argument's sake, let's say that you're going to spend an hour a day on expert-building activities. What do you plan to do for that hour each day? Switch it up— vary it. Make it fun for yourself.

I recommend that you plan to study for X hours every week. This is where you read and absorb everything you can get your hands on. Don't think of this as studying for a test— think of this as gathering materials that really interest and delight you and that you'll want to read anyway— especially because you have such strong goals and passions in mind.

I also recommend that you practice for X hours every week. What can you do to put what you're studying and learning into practice? Can you run a case study where you try different things? Can you get out there and apply what you're learning in some other important way?

Also, plan to interact with others for X hours every week. This can be online or offline— do what works for you and what fits into your schedule. You can work with other experts or other learners, or both. Get a coach or a mentor if that will help you— someone who will help you stick to your schedule so you can achieve your goals. Sometimes, it's hard to stay on track when you're the only one driving yourself. It gets a lot easier if you have an accountability partner. Announce your goals to someone else who can help you stick with it.

This may be something you want to save for a couple of weeks after you've gotten your momentum. But you should consider setting aside X hours each week to teach, write, or produce in some way. You'll learn a lot by teaching. There are people out there who know less than you do and who will want to learn from you. Teaching in some capacity is a great way to propel yourself to expert status— both in your eyes and the eyes of others.

This will also give you excellent feedback as to your own progress, because almost certainly your student(s) will ask questions, perhaps questions that you haven't thought of, and you might have to research for the answers to them. That's another way where your expert status will zoom upwards quickly.

There's no shame in saying "I don't know the answer, but I'll find out and get back with one" and doing that.

There may be other things you want to plug in on your path to becoming an expert. Brainstorm and figure out what this mean for you. I think you'll be pleasantly surprised to find that you get really excited about this process. Finally, this isn't just something you're planning to do, this is something you're actually doing!

Some people want everything laid out for them. I purposefully gave you the flexible version first. You can literally make your schedule into anything you want it to be. But I realize that some reading this will want something more concrete—something that you can start with until you're comfortable making your own schedule. So, take what's coming next with that in mind. I'm going to give you some examples of what you can plug and play into your own schedule.

For example, you may want to study for 30 minutes a day. This means reading, or watching, or listening to material that will enhance your study. I really recommend 60 minutes, but 30 minutes is good enough for a start. So, that means you should have 30 minutes X 7 days on your schedule. Adjust if you plan to take a couple of days off.

You may want to work with an expert 3 hours per week. Drip those hours throughout your week or spread them out as you see fit.

You may want to practice for 30 minutes a day. Have 30 minutes X 7 days on your schedule.

It all comes down to one of my favorite topics, which is incremental progress. Each day you are doing at least one or two things to move you forward towards your goal of becoming an expert on your topic. One, two, three steps forward, and before you know it, you've gone a long way, and it will seem almost effortlessly.

It can really help you to put the specifics of what you plan to read, study, or do on your schedule. That can really help you. For example, maybe you read Book A for the first week and Book B for the second week. Maybe you do Practice Type A on Mondays and Practice Type B on Tuesdays. Again, do whatever works for you. You'll be a lot more likely to stick with it if you're very specific, however.

Don't forget to schedule time in where you teach or produce. Again, this might be something you hold off on until you feel more comfortable. Just don't feel like you have to be the top expert in the world to start writing or producing, however. Remember that as long as you can help people who are newer than you, then you are more than ready to create something that will help them learn. Writing and producing will help you and it will help the people you're trying to reach. Maybe you want to write or produce for 5 hours each week. Work in chunks or sprinkle that time throughout your daily schedule— just get it on your schedule somewhere.

As you're doing these things, you need to have solid goals and objectives in your mind. Don't put something on your schedule just to put it there— put it there because it will help you achieve your goal of becoming an expert. Put it there because you're very clear about how it will help you. This is all part of having a solid plan that you follow through with, a little bit each day.

You can adjust the schedule up or down as you see fit. Maybe you've only scheduled one hour a day on expert building activities because you think that's all you have time for right now. But, once you get started, you realize that you love your topic and your progress so much that you want to ramp things up. Add another hour on there and see where that gets you. Up to a point, the more you do each day, the better your results will be.

It might also be the case that your eyes are bigger than your stomach. You think you can get 5 hours of work and study done each day. In reality, you just can't. You find yourself getting stressed out or even shying away from your expert building activities because it's just too much. It's okay to admit that there is just too much on your plate right now and that you need to scale things back. You absolutely can get 30 minutes or 60 minutes done on this each day, no matter who you are or how busy you are. You have time for the things you make time for. I don't care if it's 10 minutes a day— you'll get a lot further that way than you would with zero effort because you've overwhelmed yourself.

It's hard to stick to, but slow and steady really does win the race. Create a schedule, right now, that will work for you. You can consult the sample 30-day plan

I've included for you at the end here. It's time to get excited, because with a little bit of daily effort, you'll find that you can quickly become a top expert much more quickly than you ever thought you could.

Getting People to Look at You as an Expert

I've already mentioned that you probably do not want to be an expert just for the sake of being an expert. You want to be an expert because it will help you achieve a certain goal or set of goals. You want to become an expert who others perceive as an expert. You want them to look at you as one of the top experts in your field. How are you going to get them to look at you in that way?

You may have heard it said before that one of the best ways to become an expert is simply to declare that you are one. While there's more to it than that, it's not too far off the truth. In fact, there are many experts running around who really don't know what they're talking about.

Yet, people blindly follow them simply because they have declared their own expertise. Some of these people are quickly revealed for who they really are, while others are left to their own devices, misleading people for years. The funny thing is that if they had dedicated themselves to truly becoming an expert, they could have accomplished so much more.

You want to become an expert who truly is an expert. But you can still follow the advice to simply declare that you are an expert. Let people know that you are someone to follow– someone to watch. Show that you know what you're talking about and that you deserve the title of expert.

And then, of course, go out and really become that expert or enhance your expertise in any way possible.

There are some people out there who declare themselves an expert much too quickly. They try something once or learn a little something and then decide that they are an expert who knows more than people who've been doing it for years— a conceited opinion. That's not what you want to do.

In fact, I know of one Internet marketer who teaches that you can simply find a way to produce around $500 income from a relatively unknown method, and then start teaching that method to others, bringing in enormous amounts of money in the process.

I've found that it's even more common to wait too long to declare oneself an expert, however. People are afraid that they don't deserve the title. They feel like they have to know more than anyone else in the world in order to become an expert. They are scared to claim the title.

They don't realize that all you really have to know is more than the newest person in order to help them. If you have dedicated yourself to the topic and you know more than average, then yes, you are an expert. If you have dedicated yourself to consistent study and you realize that you will be learning this for a lifetime, then you'll also realize that you can, indeed, consider yourself an expert.

There is a transition period, though, when you go from non-expert to expert. You have to come to terms with the fact that you are, now, an expert. This is somewhat a change in identity. It's an exciting one, but a change, nonetheless.

You might look at yourself and think that you're not as good as the other experts out there. That could actually be true, and you might not feel like you have a right to be there in the space. But you do have that right. You are an expert and you are going to help people who want to learn your topic. You are going to achieve your goals through your expertise. This is a winning situation all the way around it– you just have to get comfortable with considering yourself an expert.

Don't Just Look Like an Expert

You don't want to just look like an expert– you want to be an actual expert to the people you are presenting yourself to. That's why we've spent so much time dedicated to the topic of actually becoming an expert. I don't want you to read this book and decide that you can just start calling yourself an expert. You need to know what you're talking about first.

I promise that if you really dedicate yourself to this, it will be very much worth it. You'll stand out in a crowded field of experts and find ways to innovate. People will look up to you and it will be that much easier to reach your goals.

Treat People Well

It's extremely important that you treat people well on your journey. If you want people to look at you as an expert, then you need to be someone they can look up to. You need to be dedicated to helping them and innovating. Keep people and their needs at the top of your mind at all times and news of your expertise will spread far and wide.

If you treat people well and are a true expert, then word of mouth will spread. It'll be a lot easier for people to look at you as an expert if other people are shouting your name from the Mountain tops. The more people you truly help, the easier this becomes. Because, in their minds, you are a top expert.

Know that every expert out there has doubts about themselves, at least sometimes. Sometimes you'll doubt your knowledge and your expertise. But it can be really reaffirming when you have people out there who are thankful for what you do... and that's exactly what will happen.

Stand Out from Other Experts

People aren't going to talk about you if you don't stand out from the crowd. They may not even perceive you as an expert if you are doing the same thing everyone else is doing.

Sometimes, this might mean being a little controversial. Maybe you take a different opinion than is popular. But, if you can back it up and explain your opinion, you will get followers. If you can argue your case, against other experts and the general audience, then you will get respect, even if not everyone agrees with you.

You'll get rabid followers because of your controversial or different opinion. Don't be afraid to go against the grain. If you know enough about your topic, it is absolutely okay to do this. It can even be very beneficial and boost your perceived expertise very quickly.

Don't be afraid to invent and innovate either. Take the common knowledge and practice out there and put your own twist on it. This is how you get instant recognition. If you find a better way to do things, share that. People in your audience will be all over it and will instantly perceive you as an expert to watch.

Constantly find better ways to do things and new ways to perceive things. Share what you know, think, and have learned. That's how you get attention in important ways and become a go-to expert in your field.

Give More Than You Receive

One of the best pieces of advice I can give you as a new expert is to give more than you receive. Think about the value you can give people. People in your audience should literally be able to get something from you that they cannot get anywhere else. If you can provide this to people, then you will instantly stand out. People will come to you again and again and will pass your name along to others.

If you are teaching people something or presenting them with something, make sure they always come away with more than they bargained for. I highly suggest you brainstorm ways you can do that with everything you do. Ideally, people will never come away disappointed when they try to learn from you.

You are going to receive a lot of value by being an expert. Becoming an expert is going to help you achieve your goals– you wouldn't be here reading this otherwise. Everything you give will return to you tenfold if you focus on providing value to your audience. Don't just think about what you are getting out of this – think about what you are providing to others. Dazzle them with plenty of value.

Have Other People's Best Interests at Heart

It's also important to have other people's best interests at heart. Think about what is good for your audience and what will help them the most. You can tailor what you teach or present to them based on what you know they need at the time. Remember that everything you do needs to be in line with your goals but think about others before you think about yourself.

Be open and honest even when other experts are hesitant to do so. Your honesty and truthfulness will stand out. If people know that you always have their best interests at heart, they will more readily follow you and tell other people about you.

This is about more than just being a nice person. As an expert, you are going to be someone in a position of power. You need to use that power for good and to help other people. Other experts may not always do that, but hopefully the ones that you follow yourself do.

Never Get Too Big

As an expert, you might find that other experts welcome you much more readily than they did when you were a newbie. They may now contact you for partnerships, share top-secret information they wouldn't share with the general public, and more.

You might also find that people start to look at you in a different way. They might expect that you know more than you do. They might lump you together with other experts in your field, even though you're very different.

You have to learn how to handle this. Don't let any success you have go to your head. Remember your journey. Remember where you came from and how hard you had to work to get to where you are today.

On your journey, you may run into experts who won't give you the time of day, especially in the beginning. That's not the type of expert you want to become. But, do you know that as your perceived expertise grows, people will be more commanding of your time. You simply won't have time to answer all of the comments on your blog, or every single email that comes in. It may get harder to keep up and get things done.

But literally not having time for every little thing is different from forgetting where you came from. Always try to help people and never get too big for your britches. If you lose touch with people who are new to your topic and your general audience, you'll lose a huge part of what makes you a true expert. Think about how you feel right now and how you would want to be treated by the experts out there.

What to Do When You're First Getting Started: A Recap of the First Steps to Expertise

Hopefully, you now have a really well-rounded view of what you're going to be doing to become an expert. Now, I'm going to recap for you some specifics, in case you haven't gotten started yet. If you already have, or if you've already devised your own ideas based on what you've read so far, then you may ignore this section. We've also already covered most of this, but I wanted to put it here as sort of a call to action.

Let's start easy. Find top blogs in your field and subscribe to them, so that you get an email every time there is a new post. Sign up for something like Google Alerts and put in keywords and phrases related to your topics so you're automatically alerted to new content based on your interests.

These are great ways to automatically stay on top of your topic, without much effort. If a new blog post by a top expert lands in your email inbox, you are a lot more likely to read that blog post than you would be if you tried to remember to go out and find it yourself.

Now, purchase between 3 and 10 books related to your topic. Choose books that excite you and are written by top experts. You'll read a little bit of a book every single day. Reading books is a wonderful way to get a variety of viewpoints, facts, and opinions.

Find and subscribe to relevant YouTube channels and podcasts. When you subscribe, you'll be automatically notified when new videos or audios are posted. This is a great way to set yourself up for success. You might also find and watch or listen to the ones that are specific to what you're trying to learn. Consume a little bit each day, and you'll be well on your way.

Also, find opportunities to work with other learners, whether that's joining forums or social media groups or finding offline groups that meet in person. You can ask questions and answer questions of these learners and other experts. You'll become perceived as an expert the more you learn and share.

You might also take this time to find a coach or a mentor. Generally, this will cost you some money— sometimes a large amount. Be prepared for that. You might just want to research the possibilities for now and make the decision on when you might take this step.

Set some goals for yourself to start teaching or releasing some content to others. You might start writing a blog at first and then move along to writing your own book, or creating videos, or hosting teleseminars, webinars, Google Hangouts, or seminars. Believe it or not, it is really not that difficult to write your own book or create your own content. Create projects for yourself that help others and break down what you need to do to complete them into neat little daily tasks.

Hosting the teleseminars, webinars, or Google Hangouts can be as simple as finding an expert to interview, and then chatting with him or her at a convenient time, then uploading the videos to YouTube, or the audios to a podcast, and linking to them from your blog.

Have you completed the steps above? Now's the time to do it. Get everything in place so you can start to take action right away. If you are going to call yourself an expert in 30 days, then you need to put in the effort. These steps will help you get there. Dedicate yourself to this with passion so that you can reach your goals.

Networking as an Expert

A very important part of this is networking as an expert. Remember that you want to become known in your field. You want other experts to consider you an expert. You want some of them to turn to you when they have questions on topics related to your specific area of expertise.

There's a phenomenon where the more you associate with other experts, the more you are perceived as an expert yourself. In fact, if you could get a few experts to declare that you're the next best expert that people need to watch and follow immediately, others would instantly perceive you in that way— it's instant credibility. That's the power of association. It wouldn't matter what you actually know, only that other people who are known have vouched for you.

You can very easily and quickly breakthrough in any field in this way. Rub elbows with other experts, get to know them, help them out, and become one of them. If you partner up with other experts, write guest blog posts for them, are mentioned by them, network with them, and develop relationships with them, they can help you in major ways.

You have to go about this strategically. Experts are not going to take you under their wing simply because you have asked them to. You have to get to know them first and they need to get to know you. That's why I've given you the advice to join their forums and groups. Take them up on their coaching. Do whatever you need to do to organically start a real relationship with them.

Remember that you can become perceived as an expert simply by association. That's why you may want to find and join mastermind groups on your topic. In mastermind groups, you'll find people who are on your level, above, and below. This is simply invaluable as you're learning your topic. Don't work in a vacuum— work with others in any way you can, and masterminds are one of the best ways to do that.

Another way you can network and get to know people is by joining groups online and in person. We've talked already about mastermind groups, forums, and social media groups online. Join groups where you can get high visibility and quickly showcase yourself as an expert. There are an incredible number of great groups out there that will help you in this area.

You can also network by starting to teach or coach others. You can become a great teacher or coach very quickly. As long as you know your topic and are willing to help others, you will be a fantastic teacher who helps others reach their goals. At the same time, you'll be getting to know people and networking. The more people you are in contact with in the role of expert, the better.

One of the most important things you can do as a networking expert is to start your own email list. Whether you're are a businessperson or marketer or not, having an email list is a great thing. Regularly mail people. Encourage them to write you back with questions and comments. Soon enough, many of the people on your email list will begin to feel like family. You never know who you're going to meet this way. You'll meet other experts and people who perceive you as their favorite expert. Having an email list is a fantastic thing and is essential when you're networking as an expert.

Another thing you can do is seek out opportunities to be interviewed. Say yes when people ask to interview you. People who are interviewed as experts on a topic gain instant credibility. You can really help people and make fantastic connections by doing this. You might even start your own YouTube channel or podcast and interview other experts– remember, knowing experts increases your perceived expertise, simply by association.

Essentially, you want to rub elbows with as many experts on your topic as possible. You'll quickly find that this instantly propels your own expertise and how other people perceive you.

Marketing Yourself as an Expert

In addition to networking as an expert, you also need to spend a lot of time marketing yourself as an expert. Of course, this will only come after you have already become an expert. You won't need to put this on your schedule quite yet.

However, my plan has you assuming a certain level of expertise after 30 days. After the 30 days, you may want to start marketing yourself as an expert. This can help you achieve your goals much more quickly because other people will see that you're an expert. Remember that 1-10 expert scale— you'll already be well on your way up the scale at the end of 30 days with the intensive schedule I've planned for you.

These days, much of marketing yourself as an expert will happen on the web. It doesn't matter whether your business is going to be web based or not. It doesn't matter if you are even currently considering running a business. Whether you are studying to become an expert for your job, business, or for another reason, having a presence online that showcases your expertise can do a lot for you.

When you're applying for a new job, for example, many employers research you on the web. If you have a web presence and it's clear you know what you're talking about, you're a lot more likely to get hired.

Whatever presence you develop on the web, you need to make sure it's in line with your goals. Consider what you want to accomplish and the audience you want to reach. Make sure that the steps you take to market yourself, on the web and off, are in line with everything you want to accomplish. This will be even more important for those who do plan to have a business, especially a web-based business.

The goal is that people should "run into" your expertise all over the web. Eventually, people shouldn't be able to research a topic without finding something you have created and put up there. Whether it's something you've written, a video you created, a group you're a member of and have posted to, or any other type of content or presence. Your goal is to become ever-present for the topic you're targeting.

By showcasing your expertise and marketing yourself on the web, people are a lot more likely to perceive you as an expert. Many people don't even realize that you can publish your own books on Kindle or other places, for example, which gives you an instant boost in credibility (only if what you publish is high quality). If you are a published expert who is active on the web, you can easily gain a following. But it takes a lot of time and patience.

When you're ready for it, I highly recommend that you add "marketing yourself as an expert" to your daily schedule. If you do a little bit of this each day, your efforts can really pay off over time. Next, we'll talk about other specific ways to market yourself on the web.

Creating a Website or Blog as an Expert

I've already mentioned that having your own blog is one of the best ways to show off your expertise and gain a following. Your blog can serve many different purposes. You can use it to share high quality content related to your topic that will help people. You can also use it to interact with people in your audience. The more you develop relationships with people, the more likely they are to perceive you as an expert.

You can also use your blog to rank in the search engines like Google. Ideally, when people search for topics related to your area of expertise, you want them to come across your blog posts. Hopefully, they will subscribe to your blog, join your list, or take some other kind of action that keeps the relationship going. You want to stay at the top of their mind, and having an active blog is a great way to do that.

We also talked about the importance of having an email list. If people are consistently getting emails from you as an expert, you will stay at the top of their mind. If you put an opt in form on your blog and give them something for free so that they'll be enticed to sign up, you can then write them with information, offers, and more. The focus of your email list should be the relationship, of course.

You can also start to develop relationships with other experts by linking to their articles and comments on the web. Experts, like anyone else, like to have their ego stroked. If you link to them, it will show up in the dashboard of their blog and it will help you get on their radar. Networking and creating relationships with other experts and people in your audience is extremely important. Having a blog of authority gives you a leg up on the competition and can help you achieve your goals, whatever they are.

You should also link your blog to your social media, books, and other types of content you put out there. Ideally, your blog should help to brand you as an expert and should list what you have accomplished and planned. For example, if you have an upcoming in-person seminar, or webinar, or book coming out, people should be able to find information about it on your blog.

If you are web savvy, then you may want to go ahead and buy a domain name and hosting account and set up a WordPress blog on your own domain. You can configure your blog in any way you want to— every detail can match who you are as an expert.

If you're not at all web savvy, don't let that hold you back. These days, there are easy options for everyone. You can simply set up a WordPress.com blog, a blogger.com blog, or a Weebly.com website without having to know a single thing about setting up a blog or website. Best of all, these options are free. Note that having a paid domain name and hosting does look more professional and might be more in line with who you are as an expert. You can pay someone to help you set up the paid option, if that's the route you want to take.

Being Present on Social Media

Social media is absolutely essential these days. It doesn't matter who you are or what your topic is, the chances are extremely high that at least part of your audience hangs out on social media. I'm talking about Facebook, Twitter, LinkedIn, Pinterest, Google +, and more. If your audience is there, you want to be there. If there are other experts dominating the space, you want to dominate it as well. That's why having a presence on social media is so crucial.

Social media can help you get the word out about your activities and expertise. You can use it to network with other experts and the people in your audience. You can also use it to talk about the projects you have going, the things you have written or created, and your audience. You can also learn a lot via social media, from your audience and other experts. You should definitely share helpful information, since that will help you get noticed as well.

It's important to realize that there are different ways to use each social network. Start to research experts related to your topic who are using these platforms. Take notes and figure out what you like and don't like about their strategy. Examine what is and is not working for them. Why are these experts using these social media platforms in the first place? Figure that out and it will go a long way toward helping you devise your own strategy.

Here are some specifics for different social networks:

Facebook –Facebook is a fantastic platform to use as an expert. Facebook is also very flexible. You may have a personal profile already. You probably won't be using that as part of showcasing yourself as an expert, though. You probably will use Facebook pages and Facebook groups instead. There are differences to each of these, so let me explain further.

You can create a Facebook page based on yourself, your business, or the topic you're interested in. I recommend you choose a focus that people will become fans of even if they don't know who you are yet. If you are an unknown right now, it might be difficult to get fans for yourself. It can be a lot easier to get fans for the topic you're interested in.

For instance, if I were brand-new, I wouldn't necessarily create a Dennis Becker Facebook page if no one knew who I was, but I might create a "How to Become an Expert" page since that's something people are interested in. They'll soon come to know my name because I run the page— see how that works?

Once you have your page created, you can share helpful links, great information, and more. Build your relationships and really impress people with your expertise. Note that I'm not saying to never create a name-based Facebook page – they're excellent for long-term branding. You can have more than one page, so don't feel like going for one excludes the other.

You can also create a Facebook group. Becoming the leader of a Facebook group is fantastic for you as an expert because it helps bring people with similar interests together. Being the leader of an active, topical group instantly puts you in the role of expert in their minds.

You can create a public group, closed group, or a secret group on Facebook. The option you choose will differ depending on your goals. I have a wonderful Facebook group called The IM Inside Track. This is a group of thousands of like-minded business and marketing fans who want to interact with one another. People get to interact with me, many other experts, and many other learners on their topic.

I suggest you take a look at the Facebook pages and Facebook groups that have already been created around your topic. Look at how the experts who run pages are using them to achieve their goals and help others. Take notes on what you might do when it's time to start your own Facebook page and Facebook group.

LinkedIn— If you're in a business-to-business field, then you should be using LinkedIn. At the very least, you should have a LinkedIn profile. You may also want to consider starting or joining groups on LinkedIn. Being active on LinkedIn is an incredible way to quickly become perceived as an expert and business and some additional topics.

Pinterest and Instagram— If you are an expert in something like fashion, or cooking, or another visual field, then you may want to consider using Pinterest or Instagram. Again, scout out how successful companies and experts are currently using Instagram to get an idea of how you should use it. You can share pictures from around the web, create your own pictures to share, and more. The idea is that you want people to turn to you first in these visually oriented fields. These social networks help you do that.

You can absolutely use social media to market yourself as an expert. Perhaps more than that, you can use social media to connect with other experts and find an audience. You can use social media to help grow your list, get more traffic to your blog, sell your products and services, and more. Many people feel like they have to depend solely on Google for traffic and attention. These days, you'll probably have even more success by using social media. Pay attention to it, look at how other experts are using it, focus on relationships, and come up with a strategy.

Writing Books and Creating Content

I've mentioned this a few times by now. As an expert, no matter what your goals are, I highly suggest that you at least consider writing a book or creating some other type of content for people to learn from. You might sell what you create or use them for another purpose. The point is that people will come across them and will instantly know that you're an expert.

Besides selling the content or using it for traffic, you can grow your email list (which I recommend all experts have) by giving away books for free. Brainstorm other ways you can use the great content you create. Remember that everything you do should fall in line with the goals you've set for yourself and your whole purpose for wanting to become an expert.

You have to show off your expertise somehow, or you won't get any notice. Someone who writes a book on a topic or has a podcast related to a topic, is almost automatically seen as an expert, regardless of how expert they really are. As a true expert who really cares about your audience, you owe it to them to create great content. You'll also learn a lot about your topic and about yourself the more you create.

This, in my opinion, it is something many experts are forgetting or neglecting. They know a lot about their topic, but they neglect to create anything related to that topic. If you want to have a say in your field, this is what you need to do. If you want to teach and help others, creating and sharing is what you need to do.

Besides that, it can be a lot of fun to create. It's not as intimidating as you think if you break your content and projects down. There are different reasons you might want to write a book than the reasons you might have for starting a podcast. You have to figure out what you most want to create and what will serve your audience best.

I suggest you go to Amazon.com and browse through the books, Kindle books, and other products that have been published on your topic. Pay particular attention to the books that have been self-published. Download these books and think about whether you could do something like that.

It is extremely easy to publish books on Kindle and other platforms to help showcase your expertise. It is still extremely impressive to most people when someone has a book published on a platform like Amazon. If you want to instantly boost your credibility, writing a well thought out book and putting it up for sale via Kindle is a great way to go about it.

All you really need to do is write about your topic in a Word document. Write something valuable that approaches your topic in a whole new way. Then, you just have to create a cover, or have it created for you, and format the book for Kindle.

By the end of the day, or the end of the week, or whatever deadline you have set for yourself, you can be a published author. This does wonders for your perceived expertise. Again, you'll also learn a lot about your topic in the process of writing about it. I'm not saying you should throw junk up on Kindle— focus on quality and helping people by sharing your unique insights.

You can do the same for a podcast. All you have to do is speak into a microphone, record it, and upload it. Let's say you wanted to do a 20 minute or 30-minute podcast. Start by writing your topic down and creating an outline for yourself. Download and use a program like Audacity, and just let the words flow out. Speak on topics that are interesting to people and create a website that features your podcasts. Submit your podcasts to sites like iTunes— there are many other podcast directories out there as well. Your listening audience can take off before you know it. This is extremely valuable content that will be listened to by the people of your audience for years to come.

It's the same for creating your YouTube channel. You can easily create videos on a variety of topics, and in a variety of ways. You can simply do talking head videos, where you use your Webcam and speak facing your computer. Or, you can use your Smartphone to record yourself doing things. You can use screen capture software if you want to capture something from your computer screen.

The more content you create, the further your expertise will spread. If you have books out there on a variety of topics, or a long-running podcast, or a YouTube channel filled with videos, you can bet the people are going to perceive you as an expert. And I can't stress enough that you'll learn so much more about your topic if you are also creating content within your topic. In my opinion, top experts create, and they create consistently.

It's time for you to get over your fear of creating. Don't feel like you have to hold yourself back until you know everything there is to know about your topic. Start creating now. Start writing your book now. You can even document your progress as a relative newbie and show your quick escalation to expert.

Document this on YouTube, or by writing a book, or by starting a podcast. People will be interested in your journey. They will even be interested in your journey as a newbie because that is where they are themselves right now. They want to know that they can do it too. They want to know that they can learn as much as you have learned. You can quickly go from newbie to perceived and actual expert if you follow this path.

Speaking at Seminars

So many things are done online these days, but you can't forget that there is a whole offline world out there. There are probably a whole host of seminars and meetings out there related to your topic. If you can become a featured speaker at these seminars, you will gain a lot of respect.

How can speaking at seminars help you stand out? For one thing, not every expert is going to speak publicly about their topic. Many people are scared of public speaking. Even if you're scared of public speaking right now, you can quickly ease yourself into it. You can start by speaking in front of small groups and working your way up.

Think about the seminars you have attended. You were probably in awe of the speakers. Even if the speakers were relatively new, you probably didn't even think about it because they had real value to share with you. That's why it is absolutely a good idea for you to become a speaker. You have a lot of value to share with other people.

Running or speaking at seminars can be as simple as joining or creating a meetup group that features them. Or, you can try to get on the roster of a large seminar related to your topic. People who speak at seminars and at other venues are perceived as experts— full stop.

Associate with Other Experts

Once again, we're going to talk about how important it is to associate with other experts. You already know the theory behind it– now it's time to put it into practice. You need to associate with experts who are already very popular with the audience you are trying to target. This will instantly catapult you into the realm of expertise by association.

How do you go about this? You have to network with top experts. You have to make a concentrated effort to introduce value to them and to the audience in general. If you want them to pay attention to you, you can't be like an annoying puppy yapping at their feet. You have to prove yourself a little bit first. Develop unique insights and show that you have something to offer

Do your best to find and create a space for yourself. Maybe it's joining a group they run and becoming perceived as a helpful expert overtime. Maybe it's working as an intern or apprentice of an expert. Sometimes, you have to do the work upfront in order to reap the rewards. If you focus on this, you can very quickly see the results over time.

Your Plan for Marketing Yourself as an Expert

You've spent a lot of time working on yourself to become a true expert (or you will over the next month). But it won't pay off and help you achieve your goals unless you have a solid plan for marketing yourself as an expert. Other people need to know about your expertise— you need to help them and provide value to them. At least, that's how it works in most areas of expertise.

What are you going to do to market yourself as an expert? Not all of the ideas will work for you, but many of them will. It might seem overwhelming by now, but it won't be if you break it down and stay confident. Start interacting with other experts and people in your audience on social media. Spend an hour or two everyday marketing yourself as an expert, once you achieve that expert status.

Focus on getting your name out there and rubbing elbows with people. You want to start developing relationships that can help you. Go ahead and draft a rough plan for yourself right now.

Plan what you're going to do, who you're going to interact with, and more. If you haven't yet investigated the top experts in your field, do so now. Make a plan for getting to know them and developing relationships with them.

You aren't stalking them if you plan strategically and work on marketing yourself as an expert a little bit each day. Once you do become an expert, you will very quickly see results because you'll have a lot of value to add to the space. Your relationships are something, like your expertise, that will build up over time with some dedicated effort.

Use Your Expertise to Create Your Own Opportunities

As an expert, many more doors are going to open for you than you ever thought possible. You're going to be able to do things that were just a dream of yours a short time ago. With this 30-day expert building plan, you'll be creating your own opportunities before you know it.

My advice to you is to not let anything hold you back. Don't feel like you have to sacrifice anything or put anything off that you want to do. This is your life, and you get to live it the way you want to. You get to create your own opportunities and create your own path. What are you going to do differently now that you're an expert?

You have a set of goals already. You've revisited those goals on a regular basis– hopefully you've revisited your goals every day. I want you to keep up with your goals. It's okay to change them as you learn and grow. What you need today might be different from what you need later on. But don't switch things around just because you're not sure what you'll achieve. If anything's standing in your way at all, you have to create your own opportunities.

The fact is that doors will open for you that you never even dreamed about before. You can't exactly predict how you'll feel after you've achieved expert status. Maybe you set the goal of getting promoted in your job. But now that you have learned how other experts live, maybe you want to form your own business now. You will change, learn, and grow as a result of this.

Maybe you never saw yourself as a coach or teacher. But now that you've acquired expertise, you want to teach and interact with others to share what you know.

Never say never, and never be afraid to create your own chances in life. The specifics depend on what your topic is, what your personality is, and what your ultimate goals are. Just keep an open mind and remember that anything is possible.

Forming Your Own Business as an Expert

I've had my own business for decades now, so I tend to see things in this way. In my opinion, absolutely anyone can start their own successful business, especially with the Internet at your fingertips. If you want to earn more money or change more things in your life, and you feel like you are at a dead end in your current job, then this might be the path for you.

My personal path to my first business of my own was a consulting practice. I had developed expertise in a specific software product (no longer available, the company went out of business, but at the time it was very popular). I was in charge of tech support for the company that created the software product and worked closely with the lead programmer.

I was also asked to teach classes to customers about how to use the product, and over the course of a couple years, I guess you would say that I was a world class expert on how to use it.

So, one day a senior officer at a major bank in New York discretely said to me that if I ever wanted to work for him, let him know. Soon after that I made the decision that I would leave my company, start my own consulting company, and I became a contractor for the bank... and later for dozens of other companies, large and small, all across the U.S. and Canada.

I could have just been a regular 9 to 5 employee for the software company and earned a reasonable income for several years (until the company went out of business), but I chose to become an expert on that one specific, little known and little used, product. Offering my services to clients made me a good living for 8 years, until I finally got tired of the constant travel.

Your business can be anything you want it to be. Maybe you want to consult for others like I did. Perhaps you want to freelance and use your skills and expertise in that way. Maybe you want to be free to create and explorer so you can travel and live life on your own terms. Forming your own business can help you get to wherever you want to be. Maybe you just want to create info products about your topic.

Regardless, your newfound expertise can help you do this. You can more easily get clients and customers if you're already perceived as an expert. You can break through much more easily if you have already networked with other business owners and experts.

With your own business, you can really paint whatever kind of life you want to have. Open your mind to this idea if you feel that it is at all right for you.

In my case that I mentioned above, I was an expert on that software product, but at the time I was very timid about marketing myself, and if I would have had to rely on my sales ability, I would have quickly starved after my first client no longer needed my services.

But I did things to position myself and make myself known, such as writing a book about the product and speaking at seminars, so that other users of that software product knew that if they needed help, they could count on me.

If you're not sure what kind of business you should start, look at the businesses other experts have created. What are they doing? How and why are they so successful? Do they work in a job or do they work for themselves? There's no right answer here. Maybe you do want to stay in your job and it truly is the life for you. This is your life– and you only have one to live. You may as well live it doing what you love to do.

Consult for High-End Clients

Many experts are called upon to become consultants. There are many businesses and people out there who don't know the first thing about your area of expertise. Yet, they need to hire someone who can help them in that area of expertise. You would be the perfect person for this role.

As a consultant, you would help people achieve their desired result. You are now perceived as a top expert in your field. If you decide that you would like to become a consultant, which would become your own business, now is the time to do it. If you can get results for people, then they will pay top dollar for your help.

Again, I tend to shift toward opportunities that allow me to make my own rules. I want to live life on my own terms– not someone else's terms. I used to be a consultant, and there are definitely some pluses and minuses to that lifestyle. The fact is that people are willing to pay handsomely for the premium information that you are willing to share with them, for a price.

Freelance

Depending on your area of expertise, there may be many opportunities out there for you to freelance. If you go this route, you'll work as an independent contractor for a variety of companies. You can take the jobs you like and ignore the jobs you don't like. You can determine how much you charge and how many jobs you take on at a time. The life of a freelancer can be very nice indeed.

As with anything, there are ups and downs. But, if you manage yourself in the right way, you can make a great living as a freelancer and have a lot more freedom. As an expert, you get the choice.

If you like writing, then you might consider writing for magazines, websites, and other publications on your area of expertise. You can command fantastic prices, especially if you specialize.

You can freelance as a graphic designer, writer, consultant and so much more. Again, freelancing is in line with starting your own business. Depending on your area of expertise and what you want to do, it can be the very best option for many experts.

Become a Coach

The more you network with people and interact with them, the more likely you are to realize that they need and want personalized help. Many people are willing to pay a premium for personalized help.

If you had your own coach on this journey and were helped by them, then it probably makes a lot of sense to you to set up shop yourself. It can be extremely fulfilling to help other people when they're starting their own journey.

You can be a coach who meets with people in person. Or, you can choose to be an online coach. There're plenty of ways to interact with people online. You can use something like Skype, FaceTime, or even just email to stay in contact.

You could accept just one client or take on multiple clients. It depends on whether you want to do this full-time or part-time. It also depends on what you charge, what your topic is, and what you'd like to be doing every day.

Coaches and mentors are very much needed for just about every topic out there. If you'd like to pursue this option, take a look at what the current coaches for your topic are doing. What is their level of expertise? How do they conduct their coaching client sessions? How much do they charge? How long have they been doing this? You can even speak to your own coach about the possibilities, if you ended up hiring one.

Teach

In addition to or instead of coaching, you may consider teaching on your topic. There might be opportunities for you to teach in-person sessions in your local area. If there aren't any opportunities like that, you can create your own opportunities. You can often rent classroom space and advertise that your lessons are available.

You can even teach online, depending on your goals, audience, and topics. As long as there are people out there who need and want to learn your topic, there are opportunities to teach.

As a teacher, you will learn even more about your topic than you would otherwise. It can be very fulfilling to help others on their journey.

Again, think about whether this fits into your goals. Maybe you've never wanted to teach, and you still don't. But maybe, especially the more you interact with your audience, you see that this opportunity is wide-open and that you can do a lot of good for your audience by offering to teach them.

Invent

As you become more of an expert on your topic, you'll probably get inspired to improve things and invent things. You'll wish that there was an easier way to do things. You'll wish that certain methods or tools existed to make life easier for those interested in this topic.

Instead of waiting around for someone else to create what you want, you can be the creator. You can be the one who invents something to make life easier or better for the people interested in your area of expertise.

As an expert, you can easily become an inventor and innovator. You can improve upon old ideas, come up with new ideas, and bring those ideas to life.

Brainstorm the problems that are present in your area of interest. Brainstorm ways that you could make things better or easier. What could you do to help people learn the topic more easily? How could you apply what you now know for people who are new? Innovate and invent based on these ideas.

Even if you feel that you don't have the technical ability to invent something new and/or improved, if you can design it, you can pass those specifications on to someone who can create what you've designed.

Create More Than One Opportunity for Yourself

Again, you don't have to choose just one of these options. You can create more than one opportunity for yourself. If you want to become a coach and teach, you may do so— especially because coaching and teaching are so closely related. If you also want to invent something, do it.

You just have to fit everything you do, and every opportunity you create for yourself, in with your overall goals.

You have to make a concentrated effort to not only dream up your own opportunities but to follow through with them. You probably have a lot of dreams, but you only have so much energy and so much time in the day.

Maybe you can start by teaching and interacting with people who want to learn your topic. Then you can come up with ideas for what you might invent or how you might innovate.

I hope that, by becoming an expert, you're able to create your own opportunities in life and achieve your goals. If you follow through, you'll be far ahead of the game. It's something to be proud of.

Unfortunately, many people decide they want to become an expert, so they have new opportunities, but they don't actually follow through with anything. Here and now, I want you to pledge that you are going to follow through with this.

As an expert, you can live the life you want to live. You can influence people in the way you want to influence them. You can choose the way you live your life, what you do when you wake up every morning, how much money you earn, and more.

Better than that, you can influence the lives of other people in a way that changes them for the better, forever. You can make things easier and better for others and give them more than you receive. I don't know about you, but that sounds like the ideal life to me.

Struggles You Might Have on Your Journey to Become an Expert

Hopefully, by following the plan I have laid out for you, you'll find it easy and fun to become an expert on whatever topic you want to become an expert on. However, I feel like I should make you aware of some of the struggles you might have on this journey, so you're prepared.

Know that even the top experts in the world have doubts and problems sometimes. I also want to remind you that success does not happen in a straight line. You will have ups and downs.

Sometimes, things will go right and sometimes they will go wrong. Sometimes, you'll feel like giving up. You'll feel like switching to another topic or forgetting that you set out to change your life in the first place. You have to keep your larger goals in mind. You have to be able to push forward, no matter what. Yes, you'll have good days and bad, but having overarching goals can help you follow through.

One of the big problems a lot of experts and wannabe experts have is not feeling "expert enough." Here's a clue– there will always be someone out there who knows more than you do. There will always be someone out there who is having more success than you're having, even if you know more than they know.

You have to keep learning and innovating. The second you stop is the second you have failed. There's always more to know, there are always other perspectives to study, and there are other ways to do things.

The great thing about *you* is that there is no one else like you out there. You are one-of-a-kind. That means your perspective and take on things is unique. People will learn different things from you than they learn from other experts. That's a wonderful thing. They will turn to you for one thing and someone else for another thing. The world would be boring if we were all the same.

Never feel like you're not expert enough. Even at the end of these first 30 days, don't feel like you aren't expert enough. Remember that as long as you know more than the newest person, then you have something to teach and share. Remember that expertise is on a scale. If you're number 5 on the scale, then you are absolutely an expert to that number 1 on the scale. You're an expert to a number 1 on the scale even if you're a number 2 on the scale. Think of this as a continuum and it will be easier to eat for you to swallow that there are, and always will be, people who know more than you.

That brings me to my next point. Sometimes, you'll feel like you're too new to declare yourself an expert. I certainly feel that way on certain topics, even if I've been focused on them for years. But, instead of looking at other experts as competition or feeling like you can never measure up to them, think of what you can learn from them. There are things I do well and things I don't do as well. Analyze what your favorite experts do and apply what you learn to your own plans for learning and developing expertise.

Don't let other people get you down. You will run into people who look down on you because you haven't been doing things for as long as they have. But that doesn't mean that your fresh perspective is invaluable– it absolutely is valuable. You owe it to yourself to become an expert and share what you've learned with others. You have certain goals that can only be reached if you continue on your journey to become an expert. Allow yourself to succeed– get out of your own way. Indeed, you are the only one who can determine if you become a true expert or not.

There's another problem that is perhaps even more damaging. Maybe you haven't been able to find your exact niche within your area of expertise. You should be dreaming about it and thinking about it at all hours of the day and night. There has to be a particular area that you are more interested in over all the others. Until you find that, you probably won't be focused enough.

If your topic is eluding you, then you may want to seek insight from other people to find your unique angle. Otherwise, keep studying, keep learning, and stay passionate about your topic. It will come to you, probably when you least expect it.

The point is that you can overcome absolutely anything left standing in your way. You can't let anything hold you back– Nothing at all. Remember that there'll be ups and downs and prepare yourself for that inevitability. Turn to others for help when you need it. Others can help you keep going even when you feel exhausted.

Above all, make sure you regularly revisit your goals. If what you're doing and what you're learning isn't in line with your goals, then you're wasting your time. You have to have that overall reason why you're doing this, or you just won't be able to keep going.

Yes, you will have struggles. Sometimes, it will feel like it's all too much. Brainstorm, take a rest, consult with others, and keep up with your goals, and you can get through absolutely anything that is standing in your way.

Becoming an Expert on More Than One Thing

What do you do if you want to become an expert on more than one thing? It's most likely the case that you're already an expert on more than one thing. Right now, you're focusing on a particular area of expertise. You have certain goals that you want to reach within the next 30 days and over the next year. You can't spread your focus. If you do, you'll find that you just treading water and not getting anywhere at all. If you try to become an expert at more than one thing at one time, you'll probably get discouraged. Instead of accomplishing more, you'll accomplish nothing.

Your 30 Day Get Started Plan: Become an Expert in 30 Days

Now it's time for your 30-day get-started plan. I want to remind you that this plan is not the be-all, end all. This is just a starter plan that you can and should adjust according to your goals and reason why.

Over the next 30 days, you need to commit yourself to this project. It's very important that you keep your goals in mind. Every day, you're going to do things that contribute to your goals. I'm going to assume that you're going to spend an hour on this each day. Adjust this up or down, depending on what works for you. At the end of 30 days, you'll have accomplished a lot. You'll (most likely) be able to give yourself an expert label, make sure other people perceive you as an expert, and make some huge waves in your area of interest.

Day 1: Find Your Topic

Today, you're going to choose your topic. This is an extremely important decision. This can't be a topic that you don't really care that much about. This can't be a topic that you aren't going to be interested in next week. This has to be something you're passionate about.

This should be something you can see yourself dreaming about and getting really excited about for years to come (and if it's something you love, it's a lot easier to get excited about). If it doesn't fit those requirements, then it may be time to examine other options. It's okay to take a little time on this since it's such an important decision.

You might start by thinking about your goals. What is it you want to achieve? Why did you pick up this book on becoming an expert in the first place? If you can't answer those questions, it's time to do some more soul-searching. There is a reason, even if you have to search a little bit to find it.

You shouldn't just keep your goals in your mind. I highly recommend that you write them down. You should write them down in extremely specific terms. The more specific you are the better. Right now, you are focused on your goals for the next 30 days. What do you want to have achieved by the end of 30 days? Then, determine what your goals are for the next year, and beyond. What can you do to reach those goals? Which topic should you become an expert in to reach those goals?

Find other experts and examine how they do things. Have they achieved the goals you want to achieve? Take notes on them and on what you can find out about their journey.

Write down the topic you have chosen and make a commitment to yourself to become an expert on that, starting with this 30-day journey.

As time goes on, keep in mind that you may want to firm up this topic and find a unique angle or subtopic within this larger topic. If you discover a narrower topic that agrees with your goals, you'll probably find that it is easier to break in as an expert and gain an audience. Just make sure that it fits in with the goals you have for yourself.

Day 2: Create Your Plan

Next, it's time to create your plan. Look over the suggestions I've made for you. Print it out, photocopy it, type it, or write it out by hand. Go through and add the specifics of your own 30-day plan, based on the topic you are trying to become an expert in.

As you are finalizing your plan, make sure that you keep your goals at the top of your mind. Whether that fits in with the template I've placed here for you or not, you need to make sure that your plan fits in with your goals.

Today is sort of another day of preparation. If you have the time, go through and get started on the next day's assignment. That will give you a head start to get that much closer to achieving your goal.

Day 3: Locate Your Materials

Today, you need to look at the materials you'll use this month. You're going to gather websites, blogs, social media groups, forums, books, podcasts, YouTube channels, home study courses, in-person courses, coaching, and whatever else you plan to use to become an expert.

Don't just gather and decide on materials indiscriminately. Make sure that anything you plan to use to study fits in with your plans and will help you reach your goals. Pay attention to reviews, the following and reputation of the person who created the materials, and what strikes a chord with you personally. You only have so much time to study over the next 30 days. You have the rest of your life to look to the other materials. For now, just choose the ones you feel will help you the most right now.

It's okay to take some time locating these materials and going through them to decide what you're going to go with for now. Visit bookstores, browse sites like Amazon, do some searches on the web, and just really canvas all of the options.

You don't want to take too much time, though. Ideally, you'll have decided on all of your materials today. Then, go through your 30-day plan and plug these learning materials into the plan so you know what you're doing on each day. You should be so specific with what you plan to do every day that you know which book you're reading, which video you're watching, and more. You may not be this regimented forever, but you should start to develop positive habits this month. Start out strong and see how you prefer to operate overall.

Keep in mind that there are different learning styles. It might be the case that you've never thought that much about what your own learning style is. Do you tend to prefer to watch videos to learn or do you prefer to read? Or do you like to listen to audios (podcasts, for example) on your mp3 player while you exercise or do other things? Keep that in mind when you're finding materials. If you really hate reading, then don't set yourself up for failure by trying to read 10 books this month. Most people actually prefer to vary their learning materials, I've found.

Depending on how much time you have left over today, you may want to get started with the five things you'll do each day, from here on out. That includes reading, listening, watching, or combination of all three. For the purposes of this template, I'll assume that you'll do a little bit each day to vary your learning. You'll also take steps to start networking and creating. You may not do as much of the latter in these early days, but it never hurts to get started.

Read- Plan to read a little bit of one of your chosen materials. Whether it's a blog, a Wikipedia article for background information, some news stories, or a book. Depending on how much time you have set aside for reading each day, this might take 30 minutes to an hour of your day. If you have more time and you love to read, feel free to keep going.

Listen- Start to make it a habit to listen to podcasts or audio home study courses while you're doing other things. You can listen to these before you go to bed or wherever you are. Audio is fantastic because you can really fit it in just about everywhere.

Watch- Try to find a YouTube video or something else that you can watch. Ideally, you'll find a YouTube channel that contains many different videos for you to watch. You can watch the videos in short chunks of time or find shorter videos to watch each day.

Network- Start to find social media groups or forums you can join. It doesn't take long at all to find these. Start to get a feel for the culture of the groups and forums you find. Start posting- answer questions you find and be helpful. Don't be afraid to share your opinion and ask questions when you need to. Ideally, you'll check in to your chosen groups a little bit each day, building relationships a little at a time.

Create- You probably won't be ready to start creating quite yet. But that doesn't mean you can't start thinking about it. At this stage of the game, you may want to start brainstorming and writing down ideas for creation that you can revisit later.

Day 4: Set Yourself Up for Automated Success

Earlier, we talked about setting yourself up for success by automating some of the things you plan to do over the next month. For example, you should subscribe to blogs you want to visit on a regular basis to receive updates in your email inbox whenever a new post is added. You can also set Google Alerts, or use an alert service like Text Walker or Mention. Also, it's a good idea to find someone who can help to hold you accountable. In the early stages of this month, you're probably feeling really excited and you're a lot more likely to push through and succeed.

Blogs- Do searches for popular blogs related to your topic of interest. You can tell if a blog is active if it is frequently updated and has a lot of comments and activity. Search for the RSS feed or sign up for email updates. Make note of any articles you want to read from the archives and add them to your reading list.

Alerts- Sign up for Google alerts or a similar service. Enter the keywords or key phrases that relate to your topic of interest. Every time something is written about these keywords on the web, you will be notified. Experts are expected to know all of the latest breaking news and have an opinion on it. Automate this task for yourself by subscribing to an alerts service– it's free to use Google Alerts.

Accountability- Find yourself an accountability partner. At the very least, post about your plans in a forum or social group. You really want to get people rooting for you. If you think your family or friends would be interested in helping you, that's a great place to start. Ideally, you should choose someone who has similar goals to yourself. You can also bounce ideas around with the other person, which can be extremely helpful.

Day 5 through 29: This Is Your Daily Plan to Follow

For the rest of the 30 days, you'll be repeating the same tasks each day, as detailed below. This will begin to build within you a habit that will ideally carry forward for the rest of your life, or at least until you attain the level of expertise that you desire.

I don't want to discourage you, but you probably already know that you can't be a world class authority on a subject within 30 days. Maybe you don't want to be, and maybe you'll be able to attain an "enough of an expert" status within that time, but if you want more, you'll keep going beyond the 30 days, by focusing on the daily routine outlined here for the duration.

Goals- Revisit your goals for the day. What do you hope to achieve? Why have you set out to become an expert on this topic? It's fine to readdress your goals as you go along, as long as those goals continue to fit in with your overall purpose. You don't want to change gears halfway through just because the going gets tough. Stick to your most important goals so you can fulfill your purpose– the reason you're doing this.

Read- Write down very specifically ahead of time what you plan to read for the day. Do your reading for the day.

Listen- Figure out when you will have downtime or a good opportunity to listen to something on your iPod, smartphone, computer, or whatever listening device you use. Put it on the background, but make sure to pay attention to it. This is a great way to learn on the go, even if you're very busy.

Watch- Plan out what you're going to watch for the day as part of your learning. You can watch the video in pieces or set aside a specific time to go through the video for the day.

Network- Set some specific goals for networking for the day. Visit your forums and groups and interact with experts and other members of the audience. Be friendly, open, and flexible, but also have a plan in mind that will help you accomplish your goals for networking and relationship building.

Create- Plan something you can create or some way to practice that will help you become a more well-rounded expert. Ideally, whatever you create should help people along with enhancing your own depth of knowledge. If this is not a planning day, work on your creation. This might be writing, recording an audio or video, teaching a class, inventing something, practicing, or whatever fits in line with your goals.

Day 30:

Congratulations! You've made it to day 30. This is a huge accomplishment and you should be extremely proud of yourself. Today, it's time to really reflect on how far you've come and whether or not you've met your goals. Hopefully, you reflected during your daily goal phase every day.

Whether you met your specific goal or exceeded your specific goal, know that you've come very far. You can absolutely consider yourself an expert after all the hard work you've done over the last 30 days. It doesn't matter whether you spent 30 minutes a day or three hours a day on becoming an expert, you've learned a lot.

What to Do After 30 Days Is Over

Now, it's time to create your plan for the next 30 days. Remember that this is a lifelong process. Over the past 30 days, you've probably figured out what works for you and what does not work for you. It's fine to readjust your plan to suit your needs and what you think will really help you.

Figure out whether your goals have changed or shifted. Set higher goals now that you know how this process works and how you've done with the process. Keep your purpose in mind with everything you do and plan. It might be time to ramp up the amount of time you spend on your expert-building activities, or maybe you're ready to slow down a little bit. The important thing is that you make an effort to do at least a little bit every day.

Over time, a lot of this will become more habit than anything else. You'll get used to seeking out expert-building materials. You'll get excited about creating materials related to your topic. It will get very exciting as you start to achieve your goals and become seen as an expert.

Adjusting Your Goals along the Way

Remember that it's okay to adjust your goals along the way. Maybe you set your goals too high for the first 30 days. You know that now and you can make adjustments as needed. Perhaps you set your goals too low and you very easily accomplished them over the first 30 days. Make some adjustments before moving forward.

There's a reason you need or want to become an expert, so your goals are an extremely important part of the process. They'll help you stay focused on your purpose. Reflect on your goals often and move them up or down as needed.

Keeping Your Reason Why at the Top of Your Mind

It's very important that you never forget the reason why you're doing this. Keep it at the top of your mind. If you lose sight of your reason why, then you probably won't be motivated to keep on going. You're already aware that this is a lot of work. It's a lot of fun, though, if you have a great purpose that you are dedicated to. Revisit your reason why every day and you'll stay as motivated as you need to, so you can succeed and become a top expert very quickly.

Keeping the Passion Alive for Your Topic

If you find yourself losing passion or steam along the way, just remember that success doesn't happen in a straight line. It might be time to change course with your daily tasks if you find yourself getting bored. Maybe you need to find some more exciting materials or to focus on the angle or corner of the topic you're most passionate about. Maybe you need to get re-inspired by the success stories of other experts. Find inspiration from others and from within yourself and it will help you keep the passion alive for your topic.

Your Journey Is Just Getting Started

I hope you feel very excited to start on your expert journey. You really can become an expert on anything, and most likely within the first 30 days, if you follow the suggestions I've made here.

With that said, you're also now aware that this is a lifelong journey. There's never a point where you just decide that you are done learning. You're going to be learning, studying, creating, and staying on top of your topic, probably for the rest of your life. You have a major purpose and some major goals and becoming an expert on your topic is a huge part of ensuring that you succeed.